Dear God,
I'm Divorced!

Dear God,
I'm Divorced!

Sara Arline Thrash

BAKER BOOK HOUSE
Grand Rapids, Michigan 49516

Copyright 1991 by
Baker Book House Company

ISBN: 0-8010-8898-4

Second printing, November 1992

Printed in the United States of America

To my grown bambinos,

Douglas, Diane, Mark, and David—

who were

> your arms for lifting,
> your ears for listening,
> your tear ducts for weeping,
> your heart for caring.

To **Barbara** and **Tom**, who belong.
And to **Dana**, newest daughter-in-love.

Contents

Season 1: Devastation

Season 2: Deliverance

Foreword

I'm afraid I'm not as gifted as Mom with her writing talents, so I doubt I'll ever be able to write a poem or short story. But there is always one inside me about her.

I thank her forever for giving me life and for the influence she's had on my life. Mom is no mere survivor—she's an overcomer.

When I was ready to throw in the towel at the Naval Academy, a Mom missive arrived saying, "Douglas, when you get to the end of your rope, tie a knot in it and hang on. Always remember that God is in front of every tomorrow."

The inspiration for her goals, for her riding out the storms of life, has been no great secret. It is available to each of us in Paul's words written centuries ago. "I can do all things through Christ who strengthens me" (Phil. 4:13).

Major G. Douglas Thrash
United States Marine Corps

Preface

Tonight we love. Tomorrow we paint the porch. The tapestry of marriage is interwoven with the threads of loving and painting the porch. A finely tuned marriage requires a delicate balance between stardust—very special events and expressions of love that make the heart zing—and daydust—menial and major household chores that keep a family warm and together. You can't have all finish and no fabric! An overabundance of stardust creates an artificially contrived atmosphere that lacks the gutsy sum and substance to survive when the plumbing has cardiac arrest at high noon on the very Thursday that eight dinner guests are arriving. On the other hand, too much painting the porch—with no surprise celebrations, no stardust interludes—robs a marriage of spontaneity, joy, creativity, and animation, leaving it cold, mechanical, and sterile.

The required balance is a delicate art, and it cannot be learned in a week, a month, or even a year. It takes a lifetime of stretching, of growing together, of taking hold of life, whatever comes. Such a balance can be summed up in one word: *commitment*. It is an act of the will, not fickle emotions, to be united through thick and thin. How precious this glue that cements a marriage and a family when the winds howl, rains descend, and floods swirl! It takes so many years to learn to live with another human being intelligently, and it's impossible without that C-word.

An endearing couple was asked the secrets of survival as they celebrated their sixtieth anniversary. "Well, we prayed every day," he quipped. "But we cried and moaned a lot, too."

"And we touched every day, even if one of us was all out of sorts and porcupine-ish," she radiated.

"Oh, yes, don't forget the big one. We never went to bed mad! Once we stayed up for three months," he confessed sheepishly.

Then that dapper groom of sixty years winked at his bride as he imparted the greatest secret of all: "On our wedding day I told my honey that if she ever decided to up and leave me, I was going with her!"

That's *Commitment.* Viva the capital C! When the rains come (and they will), the floods rise, and the storm winds beat against such a home, it will stand, for it was built on a rock of commitment.

If commitment to God and to each other is not etched in the foundation of a family, its walls will fall with a mighty crash.

Was there not in our marriage the commitment to God and each other that enters the bloodstream, bone marrow, and brain cells? Long nights I've wondered, pondered, but I can't unscramble an egg. As I've wrestled with my demons of despair, God has assured me of his loving care through everyday happenings, his Word, and his wonderful prayer promises. How I've claimed those promises!

Devastation

Pilgrimage

Surely a pilgrimage is a journey, not a destination. And it has no conventional timetable. There is no Pilgrim Inn to which tired travelers rush to arrive by sundown or before all the other pooped people fall into the pool.

Pilgrimages are painful in that they exercise spiritual muscles grown soft with neglect. Akin to Job's passage, ours often begin in the wake of tragedy. A stinging blow falls, blood spurts, nerves gasp, muscles whimper, the heart faints, and the soul cries out in agonizing desperation! Then the journey begins.

Dear God,

Myriads of fellow pilgrims requested that I speak of my pilgrimage, Father. But so choking was my grief, and so painful were my wounds that I remained inarticulate for months. Then came that 12:31 A.M. telephone call from Diane, predicting that one day I would share my story of life-being-remade with desperate, hurting people, and confirming that deliverance from my prison of loneliness was possible.

With innumerable, shrieking birth pangs, the articulation of my pilgrimage was born at 1:10 A.M., though that journey still continues.

Dear Child of Mine,

I am your unseen companion on this pilgrimage. I am at work in you, helping you want to obey. Trust me. *Philippians 3:13*

"Just Leave Us Alone!"

Willard left on an October morn when the air was soft with Indian summer. No mere words can describe the breakup of a marriage. The longer the marriage has been intact, the more painful the amputation. There is a finality about physical death, with a body to mourn. Not so with a divorce! I tried so hard, so very hard! That painful final decision came after I had dead-ended every known avenue.

In the final analysis I alone had to make that decision. No one could have made it for me. And it was the most heart-wringing decision of my lifetime! Trying so hard to hide my pain from the children, I made comeback after comeback with the Lord's help. But one day there were no comebacks left in my bankrupt system. So I cried, "Go! Get out and just leave us alone. Just go and quit messing up our lives."

One of our sons said "Mom, throw everything Dad owns into the channel! Sink it so deep we'll never have to see it again! I'll help you!"

And when some of our friends at church heard of our breakup, they glibly clunked me on the back and chirped, "Well, Arline, if anyone can make it, you can—with that faith of yours."

Dear God, I'm Divorced

How I need my parents tonight! They would have understood that I hung in there until I feared for my very sanity. They would never have clunked me on the shoulder and given out false cheer. Rather, they would have held me tightly and been silent in their love.

Dear God,
   I never knew a church parking lot could be so lonely! I am an orphan on this earth. I cannot bridge this impassable river alone!
   Oh, Father, I can't make it. I can't! And the guilt of not making it, of having no more to give, tears at me night after night. I am so very tired. Do I want to make it? Does anyone even care if I do?

> ### My Child,
>   Look at me and no other. Depend on me and no other.
>   To my children who mourn I will give beauty for ashes, joy instead of mourning, praise instead of heaviness. For I have planted them like strong and graceful oaks for my glory. *Isaiah 61:3*

Detour

Today was the blackout of my life. I became a dissolvement statistic in the judge's chamber. How could this happen to me? I had written *Little Things that Keep Families Together*, had cherished life as it burst forth within the walls of my home. How I'd dreamed of summoning our four galloping offspring, our future grandchildren, any remaining kith and kin, and all of our far-flung friends to a glorious geriatric bash on our Golden Wedding Day, the very first day of year 2002. But this will never be! What will I do with all my tomorrows? There are no more dreams to dream. Only the pain of today.

No more running, no more pretending, no more clinging to the final shreds of a marriage that was not, no tears left, only a guilt-ridden heart squeezed dry by failure. Empty, emotionally bankrupt, my self-esteem stabbed to death, I stagger in a maze of mental solitude—overwhelmed, immobilized, paralyzed, and spiritually bereft. A hint of autumn burnishes the night air as the clock of the stars points to September, but I know it not.

Dear God,

Thank you, Father, for my bambinos coming unsummoned from the four winds to wait for me outside the judge's chamber, though I preferred to walk that final mile alone. O God, I see the heartbreak mirrored in their eyes as they try to be brave and a bit funny. How deep the hurt when human love fails! Now be on your way, precious grown bambinos, so I can collapse. I have no strength left.

It's so dark, Lord; it's so dark. Can you see me? Do you love me still—even though I have violated your standard for my life? Please don't let me go!

My Child,

I was wounded, lashed, bruised, rejected, cut off from the land of the living! In your affliction, I am afflicted. The angel of my presence will save you. In love I will carry you through this experience if you keep your eyes on me. *Isaiah 53; 63:9*

When You Feel Down

This morning I almost chuckled at that laminated prayer living on the door of my refrigerator. The unknown author might have penned it just for me.

> **When You Feel Down**
> A prayer to be said
> When the world has gotten you down,
> And you feel rotten
> And you're too doggone tired to pray,
> And you're in a big hurry,
> And, besides, you're mad at everybody . . .
> *Help!*

Well, the furies have me by the hair today. It's downright hard for my soul to sing this morning. Perchance, God has a Consolation Farm tucked away someplace in his universe for tired people whose mates have departed with a "do or die" urgency to "find" themselves—to regain their passion, vigor, potency, whatever?

I don't guess that idea is too brilliant. Who knows? We would most likely only spend our time commiserating or trying to outdo each other's war stories, rather than facing up to some of our inadequacies or flaws that contributed to this mid-life departure.

Dear God,
Father, I know someday I will probably recover my stability, my incredible energy, my capacity to enjoy and invest in life. But right now I am at low ebb. All my scaffolding has been knocked out, and I'm lying in the rubble. I'm a stranger to myself. Who am I? *Help!*

Devastation

My Child,
My rivers will not run dry. Once again your face will beam with joy. *Psalm 65*

Tension Reliever

The Danes have a secret remedy. Tucked away in Copenhagen, the Tivoli Gardens provide the greatest tension reliever since Freud defined our hidden heebie-jeebies. In this fairyland of colored lights, gardens, and amusements, you can indulge yourself in the fine art of smashing china, which is far less dangerous than smashing lives, including your own.

Isn't that something? All the porcelain rejects are sent here, and a crew of smiling Danes hang them on racks and invite you to kill the crockery with wooden balls for a small fee. In ten minutes and for only eight dollars, you feel in charge of life again! Why, there have been days I could have polished off every plate, platter, dish, cup, saucer, soup bowl, tureen, tea pot, and salad plate in sight. And God knows whom I would have named every piece!

Somewhere along the way in the bittersweet spasms of growing up, I've missed an important lesson on how to articulate aggression and channel it appropriately. Now I'm experiencing a crash course in this department.

I've punched and pummeled my cheese-bread dough, slapping it around and tossing it in the air as I yell internally and externally, "Take that and that and that!" It's a good thing the neighbors had their air conditioners running or they would have rushed over and had me committed. I've even propped up the broom and hurled mental honeydews at it as I ranted and raved about fickle affections. I've jogged until my disgruntled muscles have turned to jelly as I screamed his words at the night winds, mocking his hurtful tone: "We have nothing in common any more. Our goals and tastes have changed."

Dear God,

Father, I can't hide it from you, the times I've swum the channel night and day, hurling out the words, "Rat fink, oaf, traitor, cheater, fraud!" I can't survive this seething and festering meanness! I can't keep cramming this poison into the foxholes of my mind. I will self-destruct. Yet I can't seem to let go of it. I have given up on myself, and I wouldn't blame you if *you* gave up on me, too. But please don't. Stay with me.

Dear Child of Mine,

Go ahead, explode, blow up; it doesn't frighten me. But then, O foolish heart, simmer down and begin renewing your confidence in me. Come dwell with me, your sun and your shield. *Psalm 84*

Conditional Love

What an insightful letter I received from Mark today! ". . . I was putting the final touches on my dorm room and ran across a letter you had sent me this summer, Mom. In it you said, 'We make no significant changes in our personality unless there is great pain or loss.' How much that has meant to me! I believe a person doesn't grow much without suffering. One has to go through his Gethsemane before he can rise again. Once that happens, that man or woman can walk away from his cross free, completely validated, as did Jesus.

"I'm learning day-by-day-by-day that one must leave it with God, because he has it all planned. How many times I've had to get up, dust myself off, tell myself *'I shall not be moved,'* and then gotten on with life! I did that today when I saw Rick and Betty coming across the campus holding hands.

"I guess the most important thing I've learned is that we humans exemplify conditional love. We keep saying, 'I love you because of this or that or if you do thus and so—I'll love you if you shape up to my standards.' Mom, I know that's manipulative love, and it creates a whole bag of miseries—anger, resentment, disappointment, fear, guilt! But the giving of love freely with no thought of any-thing in return—no IFS attached—is the kind of love Jesus modeled, and people blossomed and grew with his unconditional love sprinkled on them.

"Mom, I sure need your prayers. I've set my sights on some important goals this year—and some crosses where-by I will walk away a free man. I don't want to waste valu-able time and energy in complaining and wishing things were otherwise. *In this world you will have tribulation, but be of good cheer. I have overcome the world* (John 16:33).

"Mom, my prayers are with you each day. I validate you and know you'll walk away *a free woman* from the many things that have interfered with your life. I love you."

Dear God,

How I needed Mark's words and affirmation today! Thank you for your perfect timing.

My Dear Child,
How perceptive this son, how wise! Few experience the unconditional love of other humans, much less practice it. The value of this wisdom is far above rubies; nothing can be compared to it. *Proverbs 8:11*

"Please Worry Me with It"

Grief has no fixed seasons. I've been carrying these heart scalds about too long, poking them down inside me, but they keep surfacing. Try as I may, I can't silence them. I hurt all over, as if someone had taken a sledge hammer and bludgeoned my insides. Talking is not easy; I can't verbalize this grief, this loss. In vain I try to keep my pain from showing. By chance I meet Suzanne, a friend who sees with both her eyes and her heart. We exchange small talk about the weather and our lively offspring, but she senses my unnamed burden. Ever so gently she chokes out, "Arline, there's something terribly wrong, isn't there?"

Stored-up tears course down my cheeks. She continues, "We are friends of long standing. Please worry me with it if you can!" Then she gathers me up in her arms as tears form prisms in her eyes.

With no trace of self-righteousness or spiritual clumsiness, she gently stoops and helps me lift this unnamed burden.

Dear God,
Thank you for Suzanne. One warm touch from her makes winter fly.

My Child,
There is a right time for everything. Suzanne knew.
Ecclesiastes 3:1

My Heart Told Me

October's bronze is scattered across the cemetery as I sit by Mama's grave. Untouched by frost, yellow roses from our garden glisten in my arms. Only a few short months ago, Mama, eighty years young and never ill, died of brain cancer. She'd climbed the mountains of the world, crossed and recrossed the seas and deserts. Circulating editor of a small newspaper when she was stricken at seventy-nine, she was our inspiration, our ideal. We all just assumed that she would probably die of natural causes at the tender age of 110. Why, she'd spent a month in the African bush and had her room bugged in the Kremlin only a few years ago.

As the odor of honeysuckle wafted over the Smokies and the autumn wind whimpered like a lost animal in the woods, my pent-up grief began to trickle outward, and my heart told me it was time to make my first pilgrimage to her grave. Here I sit, wrapped in October's gold, recounting inwardly the rich legacy she left us. I can almost hear her whisper, "I have everything I need." True, her cracked, earthen vessel has slipped away, but that treasure of trusting an all-sufficient Lord, who knows and meets head-on every human need, remains her richest legacy to her children and grandchildren.

24

Over and over I have asked, "What do I possess within myself that can't be taken away by any circumstances?" Mama possessed an inner steadiness, a zone of eternal calm that lay unruffled even by the diagnosis of terminal cancer.

I can still see that wicked glint in her blue eyes as gleefully she reported bouncing that infernal bedpan across the floor after they had left her on it for almost an hour. "More people have probably expired from that tool of humiliation than from their original ailment!"

At University of Tennessee Hospital, test after test was run and rerun. Tube after tube was thrust down her throat. Specialist after specialist appeared. Pain in her right side built to excruciating levels, but she never let out a whimper. "I'm just plugging along, finding out all the things I *don't* have." On the eighteenth day I met with the brain specialist in the cobalt wing before Mama arrived. She walked in with no assistance and seated herself. Regal in gait, her German genes of composure in full control, she took the full blow without batting an eyelash. "When do we begin the cobalt treatments?" she asked unflinchingly.

After Mama moved out of hearing distance, the specialist confided, "The cancer spawned from the brain is throughout her spine—lesions everywhere. She had to have been in near-perfect health to sustain so much damage without being totally incapacitated. Take her home today; let her enjoy her yard and flowers. She has so little time before she will be back to stay. You can drive her in daily for the treatments."

What a blow! I prayed so hard that she would not ask me to comb her hair that afternoon or I would crumble. Pretty soon she wouldn't have any left. I remember praying, "Don't let me fall apart in front of her. She doesn't deserve that. Help my professional calm to take over. Put me on automatic pilot until I walk out the door."

Helping Mama to bed a few minutes later, I caught up her right hand and gently held it for a few seconds. A quiet, energizing calm flowed inaudibly between us before she disengaged her hand. No more guesswork. No more painful tests to repeat. No more beating around the bush. The final diagnosis!

No specialist, however renowned, could predict Mama's tenacity of spirit. On a crisp November Sunday she celebrated eighty years of abundant living, surrounded by all four children, many of the grandchildren, and friends of long standing. Eyes as blue as the sea, infectious twitch of the mouth still intact, she quipped, "I never knew I could enjoy poor health so much." She tripped that pain lever in her brain and never returned to the hospital as a patient.

Slipping in to visit her the following Easter, I knew it would be our last visit and so did she. A quietness of eternity had settled deep in her whole being. Words were few. Pulling up Daddy's old rocker, I sat by her bed all that Sunday. How I longed to tell her everything I had cradled in my heart for so long, but I couldn't. Brushing back the tiny wisps of new hair that peeped from her wig, I took my courage in hand and whispered, "Mama, soon you'll be making that Great Journey. I've had lots of people mothering me all these years, but I want you to know you are the best! I don't know how I'm going to give you up, but I do so gladly because you are going to see Jesus and Daddy!" The radiant light that crossed her face as she brushed her cheek with my hand is etched forever in memory's tapestry.

Dear God, I'm Divorced

Dear God,

"We have come to celebrate. . . ." Bits of my heart's questioning have come into focus since Mama's May Homegoing. Tears of joy are released as I place these yellow roses by her marble inscription, MISSIONARY FIRST AT HOME, THEN TO ALL THE WORLD. Praise to you, heavenly Father, bursts from my heart as I articulate gratitude for Mama's energy, her goodness, and her eternal spark, which will forever play across the keyboard of my life.

Dear Child of Mine,

Your priceless mother was one of my choice jewels. What a missionary and prayer warrior! Strength and honor were her clothing. She opened her mouth with wisdom. *Proverbs 31:25–26*

Get Up When You Fall Down

Where can I go when life has ambushed me? When anger and agony well up inside me and whimper for release? When self-laceration and guilt blitz my brain and crack my heart wide open? I know these festering emotions are choking the life from me and grudge-itis is doing me in. I'm so tired of getting mad every day. It's so unproductive! But I just can't seem to help myself.

Mostly I stomp, rave, howl, and even shake my fists heavenward, yelling "Why me? Why me?" I forget to eat. I alternate between putting up a brave front, wearing a pasted-on smile in public, and weeping alone through the night. Often I stalk the earth and wish devoutly that my ex was six feet under. I experience an alphabet of emotions—

agony, ambivalence, anger, anguish, avoidance, bewil-
derment, bitterness, confusion, disbelief, embarrassment,
fear, grief, helplessness, lethargy, mourning, pain, regret,
rejection, remorse, self-blame, self-pity, shame, shock, sorrow—even a death wish.

Dear God,

Shakespeare voiced my dilemma so long ago, Father.
"Everyone can muster a grief but he that has it." There is no
quick fix, no magic cure, and the road back must be long
and lonely. How do I take the first step?

Nestled in my corridors of memory is simple advice the
elder J. C. Penney oft gave his employees: "Get up when you
fall down." Could that be the answer?

My Child,

Don't glorify, mull over, or excuse your lapses. Let go
of the dry rot. Then you will have the strength to get up.
I will send my Spirit to regenerate and replenish you.
But you must take the first step. *Psalm 104:30*

Miss Annabell

At the end of each semester's training of my student teachers, a bit of me quietly dies, waiting to be
reborn with the next group. These young people have a
way of opening up their hopes and dreams, and I dis-
cover all the good that is always there, though it's well
hidden in some. Their joys, fears, cantankerments, sor-
rows, loves, and anguishes become mine, too. Perhaps
I've learned more from them than they have from me.

Dear God, I'm Divorced

At the final appointed hour, I tell my fledglings about Miss Annabell Watkins, my first-grade teacher. Miss Annabell was a wee, white-haired teacher of three generations of children. She had the widest lap in Jefferson City, Tennessee. Each time the bell announced the day's end, my two best friends and I climbed on Miss Annabell's lap, twined our octopus-like tentacles about her neck, and gave her a slurpy good-bye kiss. "Be careful," she whispered, as she murmured each name and sent us on our way with an almost imperceptible hug. Her eyes said, "Take good care of this hug. It's a sacred trust."

So now I tell my students about Miss Annabell. "As each of you leaves," I say, "a twinge of Miss Annabell enters my bloodstream. Something deep inside me stirs and wants to hold each of you and give you a hug to accompany you in that fresh, unguessed-at world. But you wouldn't fit on my lap too well, and the university wouldn't look too kindly upon such outbursts of affection.

"Remember that each child is special. Don't take a child's identity from him, no matter how unacceptable you find it. Use that identity as a building block instead. The only difference between a rut and a grave is its dimensions.

"Go forth, young lamplighters. A child is a neon sign just waiting to be turned on!"

Dear God,
Thank you for Miss Annabell and for what she taught me about caring. I can see those wisps of white hair and those memorable eyes right now. Thank you, too, for all the joy, pain, and toil that's gone into this semester. Be my strength, Lord, for I'm such a leaky vessel. How wonderful that you hear my prayers and give me what I need, not always what I want. I'm still learning the difference every day.

My Dear Child,
If you let me teach you, you will continue to open many doors to your students. My wisdom will protect you and set a garland of grace upon your head. *Proverbs 4:5–9*

Where Did Our Marriage Die?

Old marriages never die easily. The bonding tightens as the years accumulate. Where did our breakdown occur? We were both participants in a holy covenant. The two of us stood before Daddy and a great host of witnesses the first night of 1952 and pledged our love till death would us part. "Willard and Arline, marriage is an omnibus in which the genes of your ancestors ride, and the bus gets a bit shaky at times," admonished Daddy. What had jounced us apart? When had love gone a-begging?

Surely God knows that final decision had not been entered into lightly! I'd hung in there long after my husband told me he no longer loved me, he no longer wanted to be married. Seemingly incurable circumstances in the business world had bankrupted his ego strength, his will to win, and left him highly vulnerable. Was I not loving and supportive enough to uphold his manhood during those long sieges of downers? But managing a bustling household and the bone-crushing load of meeting his Ph.D. goal for me—when the timing was not right—left precious little time for rainbows and romance. So he

Dear God, I'm Divorced

found them elsewhere. Snatches of love songs can still bring tears. Goblin memories attack my weary brain cells day and night—stunning, mink skins on our second anniversary when we didn't even have bedroom furniture, his piercing green eyes grinning fondly at me, the times we prayed and waited by the near lifeless forms of Mark and David, thirty-nine rose bushes left around our Pensacola patio, his gifts on special and non-special occasions. How could he walk away from such memories? You don't trample your family's heart to reach your own happiness with another! Yet he did. Had I caused this?

Dear God,

"Take away this cup from me, take it away! Don't let me have to walk the road of divorce," I cried when the breakup came. But your love was silent. In desperation I found myself praying for a fatal accident so that Grannie Thrash, the children, and our larger families would be spared humiliation and bitterness. That was a cop-out you did not honor. Forgive my cowardice.

Father, I've already stumbled, bungled, and struggled through the stages of denial, isolation, anger, bargaining, and depression. Will I ever live through this last stage of acceptance and move to uncharted territories, mourning my loss while carving new skills and adaptations out of my pain? Divorce is such a poor gift to offer you. But I do so, asking you to work good even in this.

Dear Child of Mine,

Both of you forgot to call on me for guidance and strength during those final years. You established your own set of rules. There is no substitute for my truth. By my wisdom a house is built, and through your understanding it is established. By knowledge of my empowering love, its rooms are filled with rare and beautiful treasures. *Proverbs 24:3–4*

How Do You Divide the Memories?

Today is furniture-dividing day, but how do you divide the memories that go with the furniture? When our big wing sofa exited through the front door, my heart cracked open again. How well I remember the joyful day it came to live with us. That story ranks among the all-time family jollies. We were living on a church mouse's salary at the New Orleans Seminary when we acquired this jewel. One of our sons told "The Sofa Story" to all his male friends:

"Late one afternoon, when Daddy was really worn down, Mother suggested they walk down to Maison Blanche. Of course, she just accidentally introduced him to this long, high-backed sofa which—wonder of wonders—happened to be on 'a special sale never to be repeated.' Now file that one away in your memory bank. When your someday wife wants you to take a stroll with her, beware!"

That turquoise sofa had lived right under the heating/cooling vent in the living room ever since. We often thought World War III was breaking out, especially on Sunday, when the bambinos sought to establish territorial rights for their siesta. (More often than not, Diane emerged the undisputed victor.)

There are so many holes, so many empty spaces, in our house now. But they do not compare with the holes in my heart!

Dear God,
You've promised us that you would wipe away all tears from our eyes. Father, I need room service right now! Please

Dear God, I'm Divorced

don't wait until I get to heaven or I'll faint en route. Just now my tears lie like frozen rain on my heart.

My Child,

Don't store up accumulations on earth. They could be here today and elsewhere tomorrow. Store your treasures in heaven, where they never lose their value. If your treasure is in heaven, your heart will follow. *Matthew 6:19–21*

Affirmation from Afar

I claimed God's promise from Psalm 139, my favorite, as I winged my way to Glasgow, Scotland, a few days ago: "If I ride the many winds to the farthest ocean, even there your hand will guide me, your strength will support me. Every moment you know where I am. You both precede and follow me. I can never be lost from your Spirit." Somehow I knew God would place his hand of blessing on the First World Congress of Future Special Education. (Perhaps the Lord might also someday grant me a trivial request. Could I arrive in a foreign country in the afternoon or evening rather than at six or seven in the morning? I long to get off a plane looking like an alert, spiffy American in red, white, and blue rather than a bleary-eyed soul who fell off the banana boat.)

How I praise God for guiding my thought patterns and organizational skills as I entered the international competition a year ago! Deep inside I knew we had a winner. I remember the afternoon that coveted invitation arrived. My students thought I'd lost my mind with excitement.

What a beautiful surprise to find a huge bouquet of roses, each as big as a saucer, when I arrived in my room at Stirling University. Delegates on our hall thought a celebrity was visiting. Then to hear that North Carolina drawl yelling, "Sara, Sara, where are you? Mom and Dad are waiting on you for tea, but Perry is about to hog all the goodies!" Only God could have managed to have my next-door neighbors, David Mathews and his lively crew, here, too. David was on a year's sabbatical heading up the chemistry department at Stirling.

Oh, butterflies, be still! My "Survival Skills for Exceptional Parents" was the first of five presentations today, morning three, but God's strength has preceded me and supported my voice. During dialog time a young teacher agonized, "Dr. Thrash, thank you for your carefully documented research on how the presence of a handicapped child affects the family, especially siblings. How I wish I'd heard you ten years ago; it would have saved me a huge guilt trip. I actually hated my brother for all the attention and support he received from my parents until I went away to college."

Memories of this last day of the Congress will last forever! I find myself in a huge circle peopled of many nations. Looking into their alert faces, I toss my notes on "Teaching Troubled Children" under my chair and begin: "I've come today to tell of my Wandas and Hanks and Brians. . . ." In a magic moment of exchange, my troubled pupils become theirs. Quietly I move about the entire circle, demonstrating my holding and calming techniques as I speak. With my last word spoken, delegates rush toward me and envelop me in bone-shaking embraces. Some even plant kisses on both my cheeks. How marvelous is their response!

Dear God,

Father, this has been too glorious, too wonderful to believe! How could I have succumbed to doubts and despair? I should have known that—just when I needed it most—you would shower me with love and affirmation. How precious it is to realize that you are thinking about me constantly! I can't even count how many times a day your thoughts turn toward me. So search me, O God, and know my heart; test my thoughts. Point out anything you find in me that makes you sad, and then lead me along the path of everlasting life.

> **Dear Child of Mine,**
>
> Yes, I have helped you from your earliest childhood and will never leave you. You walk in my strength. What joy I know when, in quiet conversations, you testify to others of the wonderful things I do. *Psalm 71:16–17*

"... *and* Peter"

I reach out in early-morning semidarkness and touch the statue of Peter in the Vatican on this July 4. Irresistibly I am drawn to this terminal case of flawed humanity. How like him I am—impulsive, wayward, hoof-in-the-mouth, childlike, enthusiastic with a ready-made answer! Yet Peter was the only one mentioned by name in the angel's message to the brokenhearted women on that first Easter dawn (Mark 16:7).

The crucifixion was over, the cross was silent, the disciples were crushed. And somewhere out there on the dark edge of the city sat a broken man who had dined at the Master's table. Gone was his braggadocio, his self-confident "The others may desert you, but I will die with you." The cock crowed, and an anguished look across the enemy's fires destroyed that promise.

Peter had forfeited his right to discipleship. He no longer belonged. Didn't all four Gospel writers record his downfall? Oh, yes, we always remember the weaknesses and failures of others! Peter was no longer in the company of the committed—or so he thought.

And where *was* the company of the committed? Running scared, terror stricken, hiding behind locked doors when Mary Magdalene reported, "He is alive, he is alive!"

"Go tell his disciples *and Peter*," the angels said. News traveled swiftly across those cobblestoned streets to a crushed man who, in a moment of fright and weakness, had denied the One whom he loved above all others.

After his resurrection, the Good Shepherd sought out his lost sheep and reinstated Peter. Heaven is silent on that restoration, but in my imagination I see the Savior meeting Peter and wordlessly wrapping his strong arms about his beloved child. Was that not the ignition spark for the power turbines in Peter's ministry?

Dear God,

Father, I, too, have heard the cock's crowing. Sooner or later all who belong to you hear it if they run from you. I have been on the edge of the city, weeping my heart out, feeling like an outcast. I no longer belonged! I promised, and I broke those vows in moments of weakness. I want you to be Lord of my life, but my wishbone is stronger than my backbone. Put your loving arms around me to *make* me belong.

My Child,

I know you through and through, yet I love you still. I will never reject you. *Romans 11:1–6*

Dear God, I'm Divorced

"Do Not Take Vengeance!"

My brother Glenn has had some words of discernment for this locust season of my life. At first I did not want to listen to him, much less heed his advice, even though I knew he was right on target. But his words still haunt my brain cells in the wee hours of the morning. I cannot dismiss those words. They thunder through my gray matter! Again and again Glenn wrote to me: "I beg of you, do not take vengeance! Do not try to retaliate and get even. There is good reason for the biblical warning: 'Vengeance is mine, I will repay, says the Lord.' I do not think God brings vengeance on us. He just allows us to bring it on ourselves if we refuse to heed his Word.

"Treat this trauma like a stock market loss. You bought with the highest expectations, but the bottom dropped out. Take your loss and walk away from the experience. Regrets are of no value; they merely tie you to the past. Learn what you can from the experience for future use, but don't keep looking back.

"Be fair to Willard. Pay him his interest in the house, no matter how you feel about it. Take no revenge. You'll never be free if you do! I know you too well, Sis. You can't live with bitterness as a companion. Cancel the debt. Start over again from zero, as with a cash register. Do this and you'll walk away a free woman! I'm not even going to charge you for my advice."

I confess that I was mad at Glenn for discerning my root problem. How dare he be so accurate? Alas, my darker self, which seems to have too much to say lately, was really on the war path! Still, I'm grateful for having such a comforting brother, though I sometimes felt he'd been as little help as Job's friends, who did him the greatest kindness when they remained silent for a whole week!

But deep down inside me, I know he's right. I can't live with bitterness as even a part-time companion, but I keep snatching control back from God's hands. And Satan keeps sneering at me, "See there! I told you you couldn't give up your anger. Why try?" Who can free this wretched soul of this desire to get even and make it stick?

Dear God,

Thank you, Father, for my engineer brother with his earthly wisdom from on high. Thank you for his loaning me the provision to cancel the debt and start over. Who else would have ever said, "Take as long as you need to repay me. Don't stretch yourself too thin"? You have met my need through him. You care! I know you do. When my stubborn cells forget that, send your angels to remind me, please.

Dear Child of Mine,

Whenever you think about the mistakes you've made, simply thank me for my perfect forgiveness. Whenever you think of Willard's mistakes, do the same. Glenn is right. You will never claim back lost territory through bitterness and meanness. The immutable law of sowing and reaping in kind operates in the spiritual world as in the natural world. Be not deceived! I cannot be mocked. *Galatians 6:7–9*

Missing the Signals

He was a little lump of loneliness. Lean and wiry, Len trusted not a soul. No plebe in street smartness, he'd

Dear God, I'm Divorced

grown up in Tampa's inner city, where he outran, out-witted, outfought, and outcussed all his peers! None of us could dent his armor. He erupted and vociferated with vengeance. We knew his school could no longer contain him unless someone penetrated that wall of hatred. Then one day the miracle happened.

One of our graduate students trained in psychodrama dehorned Len as he was practicing his favorite stance—a bored yet cynical look, folded arms, elbows shoving first to the left, then to the right. Cathy penetrated that reveal-ing body language, then caught him completely off guard by asking softly, "Len, why do you always walk around with your arms crossed and your elbows flexed?" Abso-lutely stunned, Len paused for what appeared an eternity. Practicing creative patience, Cathy just flashed him a half smile.

Finally Len spoke: "I go around like this all the time to tell people to lay off me and keep their distance!" Then he all but crumbled. "And I guess I go around like this because I'm trying to hold myself together on the inside. Way down deep in my gut I'm scared and lonely, and I don't like myself very much. So I put on a big-tough-guy act to cover up, but I ain't fooling myself!"

Cautiously Cathy gave Len a swift, timid hug. The dam broke, and all his misery tumbled out nonstop for thirty minutes. It translated as rejection, brutality, ego bank-ruptcy, isolation, living by his wits in a failure cycle, while starving for affirmation from any source.

Dear God,

We missed the signals. *You* never do. You take the time to find out what's going on inside people. "What do you want me to do for you?" Jesus often asked individuals.

Help me to love people enough to take the time to listen with my eyes, my ears, my head, my heart. That's the wisdom of the Spirit. How I need it!

My Dear Child,
My steadfast love for all the Lens of the world is as great as all the heavens. Let me be your refuge, for my faithfulness reaches beyond the clouds. Will you be my vessel to communicate these happy headlines? *Psalm 36:5–10*

I Don't Understand

What a wash-out day at school! The college kids had hosted an all-night whoopee next door, climaxed by knocking out the screens at 4 A.M. and dangling each other from the upstairs balcony. Shortly thereafter they fell into their cars and roared away. I did pray for their safety, but my prayers were tinged with resentment from being kept up most of the night.

Today, as I began my twilight "soul jog," I came upon an eerie sight. Rounding a curve, I beheld a drug-crazed student, laughing wildly, stretched out in the middle of the road while her two companions were urging her to get up. Suddenly a car rounded the curve, and the unsuspecting driver hit his brakes and headed for the ditch to avoid running over the girl, barely missing me by a hair's breadth. My heart bumped its way to my throat, and I can still hear the girl's hysterical sobs as her companions slapped her cheeks and finally managed to reel her off the road.

Two nights before, a student declared she was going

to fly as she leaped from her eight-story room on this university campus. And one of our special-education majors sustained a near fatal pelvic and back injury when the drugged driver of the car she was riding in hit a tree. My heart cracked and my voice choked as I met with those brokenhearted parents who came to withdraw their daughter and gather her possessions from the dorm.

I don't understand this behavior, though I guess there are no easy answers. One of the freshmen attested, "Too much freedom. We don't know how to handle it." Another confided, "Pressure, pressure. You won't believe the problems, deadlines, inadequacies we feel."

"Availability," added a senior. "It's pushed at you and you're a wimp if you don't!"

"Ego builder. Man, it turns you on for a while and you feel like Mr. Somebody. You forget as you float!"

"My folks drown themselves in alcohol. What's the difference in frying your brain with alcohol and tripping it with drugs?"

One of my students bragged that he had polished off thirty-six cans of beer at a weekend frat bash. I have no doubt he did. I listened, smiled, and then asked him to look me up when he was forty. "I bet I can outrun you," I added.

Dear God,

These students have no inner locus of control. They don't know who they are. They are dependent on their peers for their identity and worth. The student with the broken back and pelvis was not on drugs, but she was in the wrong crowd at the wrong place, with tragic results. Her whole family is bleeding. The longer I live, the more respect I have for the guests I invite into my body and mind. They become part of my bloodstream, my nerve fiber, my brain cells, my muscles, my tissues.

How I marvel at the young logic of that eight-year-old in our lab school who wistfully asked his dad, "How come a Pepsi at five spoils my appetite but two martinis increase yours?"

Father, I've decided to treat my body like a Cadillac—as it will probably be the only one I'll ever own!

My Child,

Your body is home to my Spirit. Be filled with my fullness and you will never suffer from substance abuse. *Ephesians 3:19*

Is There Life after Divorce?

When I ask where I'm going, I can almost hear God's voice saying, "It's up to you. The choice is yours." And so it is! Perhaps that old saying "Time heals all wounds" should be revised to "In your own time the wound will heal." Will I syndicate my sorrow and asphyxiate—or let go and live? O foolish, foolish pride, take a back seat!

I've nursed, coddled, caressed, and embraced my wound, getting maximum mileage out of it and making myself and others about me miserable. A couple of times, when it appeared to be dying a natural death, I administered mouth-to-mouth resuscitation, then wondered why I was batting zero.

Dear God,

Not so gently, you told me why there was no celebration in my life. When I confessed my emptiness to my pastor, he reminded me of the great host of people in our church who loved me and were concerned about me:

Dear God, I'm Divorced

"Arline, they've known for a long time something was wrong but felt uncomfortable in approaching you. You don't go to the hospital to see a friend with cancer and blurt out, 'How's your cancer?' Likewise, you don't ask a friend, 'How's your divorce?' Your many friends are waiting in the wings for a signal from you so that they may return to you some of the strength you've given them."

Father, help me to remember that.

Dear Child of Mine,

When you tear another person apart, you tear me apart also. By my suffering, you can endure your wounds. Entrust yourself to my care. *1 Peter 2:21–24*

Weltschmerz

I received a disturbing note today from Dorothy, a dear friend in a distant state. Enclosed was a news clipping—the picture of a five-year-old girl who had been born with a series of birth defects. Among them were cleft palate, only one ear, and an artery from the lung entering the wrong chamber of the heart. Michelle would have to undergo a series of operations to live. Across the top of the clipping were these words: "Dear Sara, *Why?*"

Dorothy, I do not know why, nor would I presume to guess. I am only a creature, not the Creator. One of the heart's deep questions has always been *Why?* Even Jesus in his humanity and deep suffering asked his Father, *Why?* There are no pat answers. Paul was equally perplexed as he cried out, "We don't know why things happen as they do, but we don't give up and quit." I can tell you with surety that our Father, who is no laminated God, is with us in every *Why?* No emergency, no problem, ever takes him by surprise.

Dear heart, you know of my third-degree burns when I was but three, my broken back, my weeks in traction, my cancer surgery. I've been in the arena, not sitting on the bench! And there are scars and bruises on my faith. Sometimes I've felt like my brain and body couldn't take another step. But, like a laser beam, my Lord came in the quiet of the night, the brilliance of the morning, the sun-baked afternoon, to put me back together again and again.

One of the big mistakes we worldlings make is to try to imprison God in heaven. He's on earth, too, zeroing in on the shambles we make of the universe. His glory is found in so many unexpected places. But it's much more convenient to make him a celestial being light-years away from us. We say, "Stay up there out of my affairs. If I need you, I'll wail long and loud. And when I do, hurry up and answer my prayers."

Dear God,

We sit on our handful of thorns and demand, "Where are you?" When you don't use our script, we wonder if we really want you down here in the thick of things directing our lives.

Then I remember that my Jesus was a carpenter, intensely practical. He knew what it was to get his hands dirty, to be bone-weary and hungry, to lose money, to cry, to be ridiculed and rejected. People's emotions cried out to him, and he didn't do any patch-up jobs. He made them whole!

Even in this *Why?* of all *Whys?* in my life, I will allow you to be God as I take refuge in the shadow of your eternal wings.

Dear Child of Mine,

Continue to come fearlessly right into my presence, assured of your glad welcome as you trust me. Don't lose heart! *Ephesians 3:12*

Chicago Happening

Today was gift-wrapped by the Lord! En route to Chicago, I sat by this zippy seventy-five-year-old grandmother of sixteen who had been widowed for five years. She introduced me to all twelve grandsons and four granddaughters via snapshots. "I met my husband on the third of one month and married him on the thirtieth," she told me. "My only mistake was not marrying him on the fifth when he asked me! His grandfather and Kit Carson were brothers. The descendants of Daniel Webster and Daniel Boone also lived in our community, and we pretty well ran the place!"

Reporting my arrival at the O'Hare Regency, I then hid in the bubble-domed pool for over an hour. Then, lo and behold, I was addressing all those people on "Why Is Common Sense So Uncommon in Parenting?" What beautiful rapport as I shared the theater of my mind! They laughed so hard at times, I just had to stop. Why, I had no idea it was that funny. There were bursts of applause throughout the speech. They shed a few tears as I confessed my terminal case of humanity in mothering four teenagers for eleven (going on two hundred) maniacal years. They tasted my joy, despair, anguish, and semi-permanent insanity. My earthiness, my fragility, my vulnerability, reached out and touched their tender spots. How could they know this was my valedictory to wedded life as I paid homage to the father of my children?

Dear God,
   When they gave me an extended ovation that lasted until I left the hall to catch my plane, salty tears streamed down my

face. Some caught my hand, and it was as if you had touched me, Father. Thank you, thank you that I am not a failure. I was so moved, so energized that I could have walked barefooted across the Milky Way!

Dear Child of Mine,

Don't worry about anything; instead pray about everything. Tell me your needs and don't forget to thank me for answering those needs. If you do this, you will experience my peace, which is far more wonderful than the human mind can understand. My peace will keep your thoughts and your heart quiet and at rest as you trust in my Son Jesus Christ. *Philippians 4:6–7*

Please Touch Me— Let's Hug!

What a day! Returning from a whirlwind speaking tour in distant parts, I'd promised Dr. Hugh and Ruth I'd report on my saga as soon as I hit Long Branch Hollow. Playing a joke on them, I rang the doorbell at dusk instead of going through the "home folks" entry and yelling my customary "Anybody home?"

Doc answered the jangle and just stared at me in the misty drizzle. I was not expected for another day. Breaking into that broad grin, he drawled, "Let's hug!" Then he enfolded me in a big bear hug, which added benediction to a special day. He and Ruth could make any day special!

How vividly I remember sitting with my friend Judy in a small park overlooking Rome on a Sunday afternoon,

Dear God, I'm Divorced

inhaling all the infectious sights and sounds of family life. Several small children were playing ball before a delighted audience of parents, grandparents, aunts, and uncles. One elderly gent stooped beside his grandson, showing him how to position his hands to catch the ball. Then he gave the little fellow an affectionate whack on the behind and an exuberant shout of encouragement. When Judy asked permission to take some snapshots, grown-ups rushed over to tidy up the children, give them a hug, and admonish them to stand tall and smile into the nice American's camera. Some of the more adventuresome mothers hugged Judy and me, pressing pieces of paper with their names and addresses into our hands and gesturing wildly that they would like a print.

Another time, on Embassy Row in Paris, I marveled at the camaraderie of a young father and his son as hand-in-hand they crossed a busy street. When they reached the other side, the father did not abruptly drop his son's hand. They sauntered for another block, their fingers entwined as they carried on an animated conversation.

Dear God,

How we earthlings need hugging! And we never outgrow that need for affection and affirmation. Somewhere along our way to sophistication and self-sufficiency, we've forgotten the power of human touch. We are touch-poor and suffer from skin hunger. So many of your children, myself included, wear a big, invisible sign: *Please Touch Me—Let's Hug!*

My Child,

In the long ago mothers brought their infants for my Son to touch, hold, and hug. Little children, of such treasure is my kingdom forged! *Mark 10:14–16*

Ode to My Crockpot

Wasn't it a puzzled Englishman who ventured that only in the United States would they have crockpots to slow down cooking and microwave ovens to speed it up? "I suppose the ultimate would be to fill the crockpot and put it in the microwave!" was his somewhat cynical postscript.

Maybe so—but my crockpot of earthen brown has been a great comfort. How many gallons of chili, quarts of beef stew, and dozens of pot roasts have simmered, bubbled, and gurgled within her walls? She's made the local scenes at barbeques, church suppers, picnics, and student jamborees. What a necessity this unromantic Valentine proved to be! It's been a lifesaver, allowing me time to be more Mary than Martha.

Dear God,
I know you've always been concerned about earthly things—the yeast in dough, salt, mustard seeds, feasts, new wine. So thank you for my crockpot. You are our helper in everyday, mundane matters if we really invite you to take up residence in our homes. Don't ever let me shut you out in anger or neglect. I'd fall apart without you!

> **My Child,**
> Blessed be your crockpot, which has fed the multitudes. Make hay with it while the sun shines! *Proverbs 10:4–5*

"Can I Borrow My Car Tomorrow?"

I think the spaces between my hurts are ever so slowly increasing. I can even crack jokes, like my transportation jolly tonight as I asked Dave, "Son, can I borrow my car tomorrow?"

"Sure, Mom, why not?" he agreed. "But how long do you think you'll be needing it? And you'd better check the gas tank, as it's sort of hovering on empty."

Talk about understatements! That tank had been hovering on empty for four days. Some misguided energy official in Washington is missing a high opportunity to solve the oil crisis in our country by not calling forth Dave's talents. He can run Red Whale on a teaspoon of gas for days. In discussing this American phenomenon at the local chapter of Pedestrian Parents, it seems the only time we can be guaranteed the family wheels is when the tank is gasping for nourishment.

I wonder how Grandfather Elisha Bain or Granddaddy McDonald handled this problem. Did they get the horses back from their kids only when the vultures were circling the barn?

I'm looking forward to that day when I'll be riding about heaven's streets in my chariot (or whatever) without casting a beady eye on the gas gauge.

Dear God,

How grateful I am for your storehouse of celestial energy of which there is never a shortage! Thank you, too, for my bambinos' good humor, which prevails through all and manages more and more to tickle my funny bone. Bless the Joy Boys tonight as they depart in Red Whale to see their "chicks" in the next city. Bring all four home safe and sound. Thank you for hearing a Pedestrian Parent's prayer. Tomorrow is my day with the car. Could it sport some gas, please?

Dear Child of Mine,
Be full of joy and hope! My mighty power is dealing with you. *Romans 15:13*

Seven Tiny Coins

This morning Mitzi greeted me with "Mrs. Thrash, I've waited forever for today. How come the good things in school take so long to sneak up on you?" This was to be our long-awaited shopping excursion to a large mall on the other side of town. Many of our special-ed students had never been to a mall, so they bubbled into the room in their Sunday clothes, unable to hide their overdoses of pent-up energy.

At one end of the mall sat a blind man, selling pencils, erasers, and other small items. His money cup was almost barren. Mitzi's brown eyes grew larger and larger as she pointed to him and whispered, "Who's that man?"

"Why, Mitzi, that's a beggar," I said.

"What's a beggar?" she persisted.

"Hmm. Well, Mitzi, we've talked about handicaps in class. See, this man has a handicap. He's blind—so he must sit in the mall and sell small things. But he's really begging us to help him."

"But there's not much money in his cup! Does he have another job?"

Dear God, I'm Divorced

"No, Mitzi, he doesn't get up and go to work like your daddy. This man is blind, but other beggars are crippled or can't hear or talk. Sometimes they must ask people to help them."

"Does he have a family?" she wanted to know.

"He may have a family. Many beggars do."

Without a word, Mitzi went over to the edge of the mall and sat down. Taking off her right shoe and sock, she shook out two dimes, one quarter, one nickel, and three pennies. Hopping on one foot over to the blind man, she placed the seven coins in his cup and ever so gently patted him on the cheek.

Dear God,
What a beautiful, unforgettable lesson Mitzi taught us all today! Thank you for reminding me once again how much I can learn from my students.

> **Dear Child of Mine,**
> Many children know far more about my kingdom than do grown-ups! *Luke 10:21*

Bequeathal

My neighbor died today without warning. While sailing with some of his students, Wilbur collapsed in the boat and his heart stopped en route to the hospital. How strange it will seem to look across the channel and no longer see him bending over his desk and tinkering with some model. The windmill whirling away by the seawall bespeaks his creativity.

Devastation

This afternoon I brought Wilbur's family warm cheese bread and a tiny nosegay of lavender roses from our garden. Hugging his wife, I stammered, "Oh, Helen, I'm so sorry! What a loss. . . ." Then I recalled to his parents and brother the warm memory of a Thanksgiving past when I heard the Doxology wafted across the water. Wilbur and his family, hands joined, were singing grace before enjoying their back-porch bounty. We talked of his talent as a high school bandmaster and of all the student concerts he taped and played so often. He often gave us our own Hollywood Bowl right on our boat dock.

Now, dangling my feet in the salty brine at dusk, I ponder my bequests to my offspring. Money it would not be! Would that I might bequeath them roots and wings. Roots for anchorage and depth, and wings on which to soar above mediocrity. We have known grief beyond human understanding. At times it might have been easier to give up in resignation. But love is the greatest shock absorber of all, and somehow we've lived and loved through all the troubled waters. Commitment is the glue that cements a family's roots so deeply that even the fiercest storm cannot disturb its tenacious hold on life.

When our Douglas left the family nest for the Naval Academy at the age of seventeen, he surveyed his woebegone family at the airport. Choking back tears, he called out, "Take care!" Unknowingly, he coined our family benediction: "Take care of yourself, for I love you." These simple words reaffirm our belonging, our commitment, and our love for each other. They have become an integral part of telephone conversations, letters, and farewells, along with our jollifications. "Take care!" we tell each other. "Learn to find safe harbor in the storm."

In addition to roots, I would bequeath my bambinos

Dear God, I'm Divorced

strong wings on which to soar—wings of joy, of laughter, of optimism. I thank God for bestowing on us the gift of laughter. It is the greatest face-saver and sanity-preserver known, for it dissipates pride and self-commiseration and brightens our sullen interiors. "Don't take yourself too seriously" is a frequent admonition in our family. Even after some of our disasters, we have managed to let ourselves go in sidesplitting, self-humbling laughter. "Mama, it's our zany humor that carries us beyond our miseries and over the hump again and again," a slightly bemused Diane once announced.

When someday I run out of sap and fall down like a giant oak, the eulogy at my Going to the Big House celebration will probably go like this: "Mother passed through our lives like spring wind. She was the champion giggler, sometimes too much given to hilarity, especially during prayers, in church, and on very solemn occasions. She'd roll those brown eyes and be off and running on one of her nonstop laughing sprees. Though we'd get blamed and often sent away from the table, Mom was the instigator. But how could Daddy send her to her room?"

Maybe someone will add: "Mom was a fantastic cook. Her cheese bread and New Orleans spaghetti were out of sight. But you should have seen the kitchen. Every culinary concoction left the place looking like Hurricane Hattie and Typhoon Tillie had hit simultaneously. And who of us could ever forget that disastrous snook, dressed in anemic cracker crumbs and drowned in Grandma's Barbeque Sauce? That was the only dish that ever went straight from oven to table to garbage. Though we cleared the table that night as usual, we didn't kiss the cook for her efforts. But we *did* laugh."

Dear God,

Father, if my offspring mention that poor fish at my Glory Service, may I have permission to depart my celestial home, fly down, and begin a prolonged laughing spree? And when we're limp from all our sidesplitting guffaws, I'll whisper "Take care" in each one's ear before I return to the other side of the rainbow.

> **Dear Child,**
>
> My gifts are better than the purest gold or sterling silver! There can be few more precious legacies than the continual feast of joy that lives in a merry heart. *Proverbs 8:19; 15:15*

The Getting-Yourself-Together Corner

Long before "getting yourself together" (or "gathering yourself," as the British say) became popular, I had a getting-yourself-together corner in my classroom of young handicapped boys. There was no stigma attached to being there, and even I fled to that corner when the troops became too much for me. My students and I often talked about falling apart and what that meant. How precious was one boy's explanation! "Some days nothing goes right. No matter how hard you try, the world just stomps your insides clean down to your big toe! How come most teachers always sends you to the Head Honcho's office on those stompin' days—when you're having enough troubles already?" The boys and I finally worked out a system. A raised index finger meant "I need a few minutes in the Together Corner." At first I would have to lightly tap one highly erratic little fellow and point to the Together Corner when I perceived his overloaded circuit was about to blow. After three weeks, he took over his own behavior management. Often forgetting the signal, he would mutter to himself, "Better get to the Together Corner fast!" Then it would usually take but a few minutes before he would proudly announce to the troops, "Well, I'm ready to join the human race again." What precious lessons in humanity these God-touched children taught me!

Dear God,

Father, do you think I will ever depart the getting-yourself-together corner? I've been there for months, it seems. Will I be ready to rejoin the human race before the Rapture?

> **My Child,**
>
> Life has stomped you down to your big toe, but you have good genes. You're on your way back. Welcome to the human race! I will bring great things to pass when it is time. *Isaiah 60:20, 22*

"Dear Professor . . ."

When my heart scalds become too heavy to bear, when I feel no longer able to walk along the way, my Savior comes walking on the water in so many unexpected ways and brings me peace. His latest affirmation of love came through Debbie's note today.

"Dear Professor," she wrote, "You're a wonderful person

in all the ways that count the most! I just wanted to say a simple thank you for being such an inspiration to me. During the few years I have been here at the university I have been bombarded with so many theoretical concepts that I began to wonder if that is all there is! Thanks for sharing some practical, commonsense ideas that I can apply in my field. You know kids through and through. But most of all, thanks for sharing your bright, shining faith with us. So many mysterious things happen that we do not understand. But there is a Higher Being who does understand. I am so sorry about your brother's cancer. Some professors would put up a bold front and never share a heartache, but not you! You will be in my thoughts and prayers often."

Dear God,

Father, how I needed those words today. And you knew! Thank you, too, for the red rose and beautiful note Cheryl and Mary left on my desk today. How I praise you—my professor—for my students' sensitivity!

> **My Child,**
>
> Many are the mirrors that brightly reflect my glory. Fix your eyes on me and the eternal glory yet unseen.
> 2 Corinthians 4:18

Gift-Wrapped from God

How strange was Sunday night's phone call! "I haven't talked to you before, but . . ." Then followed a twenty-minute torrent of words that spoke of unbelievable agony, deception, and broken promises, and a final leave taking. "I can't sleep, I'm cracking up, wallowing in self-pity; I can't get hold of myself. I have no self-worth. How have you managed to remain a lady all these years?" she asked me.

Old wounds, so painstakingly sutured, broke open again, but now they bled clean. No festering poison, no gangrene of anger, no raging infection. Oh, I'd been to the mat with those pernicious antagonists time and time again! Victory came only after fierce combat. Now sleep eluded me, though I had a heavy teaching day on Monday. *Will this wreckage of lives never end?* I wondered. *How many more bodies will be strewn by the roadside?* Salty tears poured down my cheeks as I prayed for the anguished caller caught in her own web of stagnation, abandonment, and pain. Yes, I could pray for the woman who had desecrated my home. It was a hard-won victory. But in absolute stillness I heard God whisper, reminding me that she was his child, too, as was the man who had inflicted the agony on us both.

A week after I'd pondered this strange call, I spoke of it to a trusted colleague. "As upsetting as that call was, it became a blessing," I said. "You see, there still remained a pang of guilt gnawing at me, reminding me that perhaps there was something else I could have done, some other measure I should have taken. But in the selfsame moment —as I told my night caller that nothing *she* did or did not do would have altered the situation—I knew of a certainty that this was also true for me. Even though the children had told me over and over the same thing, I could not believe it. Now I am set free."

"Sara, you're so right, you're so right!" smiled my friend. "That message was gift-wrapped from God in a strange package. And, as always, his timing was flawless. Not a minute too early nor a minute too late! Think now—had that call occurred eighteen months or even a year ago, you would not have been ready to receive or believe it. You were still torturing yourself with all those 'maybes.' But time and grief's slow wisdom have disposed of those doubts, one by one, and you were ready to receive the gift. Remember that true forgiveness begets receptivity. Your willingness to accept and forgive this detour in your life has hastened your passage to freedom."

Dear God,
Thank you for your gift-wrapped message. I can now gently close the door on my sad memories and not look back. I am free to remake my life according to your purposes. Will you show me the way?

My Child,
Why try to understand everything that happens to you? Trust me with all your heart. If you acknowledge me in everything, I will direct you. *Proverbs 21:1–2*

Deliverance

Good-bye, Pity City

What marvelous things happen when we lift our frail, sagging lives up to the light! Now I have this Visiting Professorship of Special Education at St. Leo College. I had but one more house payment in my coffers, but God knew that and heard my cry for help. He is my purse keeper, too, I see. Although my salary is much smaller than a university one, every bill has been paid.

These eleven-hour days of work and commuting leave no room for Pity City mentality. Joyously I shed my exhaustion as I swim the channel at dusk and inhale the peace of the sunset. I explore the misty country of my soul, and realize I have tasted the worst and am still alive. Because I still believe, I am strong. What a battle cry!

Dear God,
Thank you for the quietness and beauty of the campus chapel, the morning harbor that banishes my goblins of the night. Each day I kneel here empty-handed, and you bend down and restore my confidence.

And thank you for the orange groves and rolling hills where I can run and regain life's rhythms, where my brain can burst from its cage of self-doubt. Ever so faintly I realize that when your children sing hymns of praise and joy, you ambush the enemy and smite him.

My Child,

As you continue to trim away the superfluous and unimportant from your life, you will be filled with gratitude and praise. The joy that I bring you will be your strength. Partake of it freely. *Nehemiah 8:10*

Potent Medicine

The hills are green and the wind is mellow on campus today. But I'm suffering from temporary mental stagnation. How I need someone to bombard me with energy. Well I remember playing that game with our learning-disabled students at our lab school in North Carolina. One downhearted student would take a chair in the middle of a circle and I would usually straighten his shoulders and beg a smile. We would then go around the circle and each person would tell the center-stage student one outstanding thing about him that might otherwise be a well-kept secret. An appointed scribe recorded these goodies on poster paper for posterity. What a beautiful sight to see a withered human being responding to the oxygen of caring affirmation!

One bright ten-year-old, an unsuccessful extrovert with an extreme case of hoof-in-the-mouth malady, once reminded us, "I know a few good ones you left out!" Another student, who had suffered through five different remedial programs at a summer reading camp, blurted out, "Would all of you please sign your name to these testimonials?" Affirmation is potent medicine!

Dear God, I'm Divorced

Dear God,
What an example Jesus set in bringing out the best in those who thought they were nobodys! Please help me to see the beauty in others, especially those who feel left out, abandoned.

> **My Child,**
> Be kind to all those in need. Fire goes out without fuel. So do my children. *Proverbs 14:21; 26:20*

What Gets Your Attention Gets You!

In the city of my birth, a sprightly gentleman, well into his eighties, keeps his mind agile by arising each morn and asking his wife, "Now what shall I think about today?" Then he answers his own question. For example, "Today I am going to think about my friends in Dandridge, Tennessee." The next morn he may announce, "Today I am going to think about all the homeless people in our cities." This former professor and administrator keeps himself alert daily with all his "Today I am going to think about someone but myself."

We are told in God's Word, "As a man thinketh in his heart, so is he." Maybe that should read: "What gets your attention gets you!" So many illnesses today are caused by emotional congestion. Ancient grudges, old pain that has never been released, vie for our undivided attention and usually get it. Unresolved anger is probably the number-one killer in our country today.

How well I remember timidly venturing forth to a conference on divorce recovery. One woman, who had been deserted for a more streamlined model, spoke openly of her days of bitterness as a walking wounded: "I should have won Martyr of the Year award for two straight years. I ranted and raved continually—a litany of 'How could he do this to me?'" She then looked around the room at all of us and continued sheepishly: "One day I woke up and said, 'Well, he did! Now, what am I going to do about it and—just as important—what am I allowing it to do to me and my children?'"

I've been there, too. But today I am also asking myself, "What am I allowing God to do *to* me, *with* me, and *for* me through this experience?" And that's where the rubber hits the road! Asking that question and waiting for an answer with all your heart, mind, and soul is risky business, dangerous to the ego. We're not microwaved through these experiences. We're slow-cooked and it hurts! So we cry out, "How long, Lord, how long?"

Warren Wiersbe's interpretation of 1 Peter 1:6–7 answered that anguished question for me. "When God permits his children to go through the furnace, he keeps his eye on the clock and his hand on the thermostat. His loving heart knows how much and how long."

Dear God,

I don't want this divorce to be the number-one event of my life! I want *you* to be that. I long for the indwelling Christ to take up permanent residence in the throne room of my life. When he does that, there will be no room for bitterness or hopelessness—for my eyes will be fixed on him alone.

My Child,

Whatever things are true, honest, just, pure, and lovely—fix your mind on these things. Attend to them

64

and put them into practice. Then my peace will descend upon you. *Philippians 4:8–9*

Polish Your Happiness Collection

What a time I had in Boynton Beach, Florida, where I escaped from my campus at spring break! Landing right side up on my friend Evelyn's doorstep, I was told I was just in time for a big Love Feast. (Although I knew early Christians held Love Feasts, my mind fleetingly conjured up a pagan orgy, with half-inebriated people tossing grapes into their mouths in between doing whatever else one does at such a revelry.)

Said Evelyn to me, as a shadow passed across her face, "We've had three family deaths within the last two years. At Daddy's funeral a few weeks ago, I reminded the family that the only time we all gathered together seemed to be to mourn a departed member. So I invited them on the spot to set aside this Saturday to gather at my house and celebrate the living."

And celebrate they did! Five generations came—from the matriarch of the clan to the tiniest toddler, who clutched at the tablecloth and grabbed cookies with his tiny starfish fingers. What aromas tempted our gluttony! Unashamedly, family members reaffirmed their love for each other as they relived event after event and replaced these priceless treasures in their memory banks.

Sadness overshadowed this merry event for me upon

returning home and finding that one of our most vibrant singles, who had just celebrated her twenty-fifth birthday, had entered the hospital for a brain biopsy. Her brother had died of a brain tumor.

At high noon this Easter Saturday we singles are having a Love Feast to celebrate God's love for us and our love for each other. The feasting will begin in my kitchen and dining room and continue to our screen porch and boat dock, spilling over into our neighbor's yard. We'll dine, recline in lounge chairs, laugh, weep, break out the guitars, and yodel as we commemorate the joys of life and polish our happiness collection. Who ever said Christians didn't enjoy hilarity? Who knows? We may toss a grape or two.

Dear God,

This Saturday we will acknowledge that we are grateful heirs of today, exhilarated connoisseurs of the present, devoted recipients of everything you have bestowed. And as that giant ball of red sinks into the west, we'll join hands and call forth an old blessing on each other.

Dear Child of Mine,

Celebrate the love of family and friends and polish your happiness collection every day. Worldly treasures sprout wings and fly off like an eagle, but words that celebrate love are more precious than apples of gold in silver baskets. *Proverbs 23:5; 25:11*

Nothing Is Unspeakable in a Storm

What a family has been bestowed on me. From earliest years I've told these bambinos that honesty tempered with a sense of humor can reinforce any relationship. But what uncanny wisdom they have developed without my help!

Son Two just slipped into the kitchen and all but lifted me off my feet. "Mom," he said, "one thing this experience has taught us is that nothing is ever unspeakable in this family again. Nothing! No matter how terrible! For so many months our eyes tried to hide from you what we saw, and your eyes tried to hide from us what *you* saw. Consequently, we all went off into separate corners and bled alone. If only we had been honest with each other, we could have thrown our arms about one another, braved the squalls together, and formed a support system. We have learned our lesson. Nothing is unspeakable among us."

Dear God,
    Father, you have told us, "You shall know the truth and the truth shall set you free." Sometimes it makes us miserable first! Help us not to hole up in solitary confinement with our hurts.

> **Dear Child of Mine,**
>   Speak the truth in love and you will grow more and more in my likeness and be bonded inseparably with all of my children. *Ephesians 4:15–16*

Bless You, Bambinos!

I would be less than honest if I didn't admit that had it not been for my children, so tender yet so tough, I would have given up the struggle for life long ago. Time and time again they've lent me their capacities and resources for survival before I relocated that precious vein of survival buried deep inside me and tapped it for faint sprouts of new growth. Over and over again, when I came to the breaking point, one of them reached across the miles with near ESP powers, stemmed the bleeding, and handed me back my courage.

Unknown to me at the time, they had formed a telephone network across the nation, and one would report to the others when I was at lowest ebb. Then mysterious resources would crackle across the wires. Months later they sheepishly confessed dispatching David to remain with me a bit after my first solo Christmas, for fear I wouldn't make it.

My first visit to Doug and Barbara's home in California proved unforgettable. After seeing their open love for each other, I crawled into bed early that first night, feeling lonely and bereft. A sudden knock on my door brought Doug and Barbara piling on the bed, a Thrash habit of long standing. "Mother, we haven't had our family devotions yet," Doug scolded. After he read the Word and prayed, he and Barbara tucked me in for the night. Barbara's touches on every subsequent visit, reminding me I was still a vibrant person, were very special. And there was Doug's admonition from the high seas: "Mother, surely you don't believe God has brought you through thick and thin only to desert you now."

Diane's organization of the networking, reporting to her brothers regularly, touched me deeply. She recognized my fierce independence yet realized I could not make it on my own. Her memorable 12:31 A.M. phone call—reminding me that I would someday go across the nation and the world, helping people put their lives back together—gave me hope and assurance that I was not a failure.

Mark's quiet attention, his gift of comforting affirmation, plus quoting my words to him during some of his own "dark nights of the soul," restored much needed balance to us both.

Dave's affection and toughness with me when I needed it facilitated the catharsis. His wiring me six yellow roses (my favorite blooms) on my birthday, though he hardly had money for himself, is one for the record book! During my third solo Christmas, he and Mark had come only for Christmas Eve and the next day. His dad called and invited us to see his house and the improvements he'd made in it. After checking with the bambinos, I accepted the invitation. Shortly thereafter, Dave strolled into my bedroom. "Mom, you're sure you can handle this?" he asked. "Yes, son, I'm sure. When Doug passed through last spring and Dad invited me to come down with him, I couldn't. It would have wiped me out. But I can handle it now." Dave smiled his famous half-grin then drawled, "Okay, Mom, just checking." Bless him! Had he not thought I could have made it, he would have insisted I not go.

Son Four, as we call Tom, remained with me when Mark and Dave had to leave on Christmas afternoon for work or school. Other times, his cheery phone calls often made my day, and his tough love dispelled any illusions of a "quick fix." When Mark was ordained to the ministry,

Tom interrupted his physician's schedule to fly in from Tallahassee. He sat on one side of me and Mom Hicks on the other, as they were my family that night.

Dear God,

When I had four preschoolers, I thought I'd never live to see their teen years. I kept telling myself, "Someday having all these urchins will pay off." And it has! How wonderful the other day to hear Mark tell a friend, "My mom's divorced, but she's an all-together woman." I'm not there yet, O Lord, I'm not. But with your help and their love and affirmation, I'm on the way. Thank you also for Barbara and Tom, who belong, too.

> **My Child,**
>
> Children are my gift, my special reward. They sit around the dinner table as vigorous and healthy as young olive trees. May you live to enjoy your grandchildren! *Psalms 127:3–5, 128:6*

"Go to the Mountain"

I'm afraid! I'm sinking again! I've run out of spiritual chin-ups. My spring and summer terms have ended, and St. Leo's has offered me a permanent position. Yet a cautionary check is audible to my inner ear: "No, don't accept that. There is something better for you. Wait."

Seven weeks have passed, and my coffers are almost empty despite my frugality. Inside I now keep hearing, "Go to the mountain." But there are no mountains in Florida. Did I misunderstand my instructions?

Dear God, I'm Divorced

Dear God,

How I long to catch the rhythm of living again! I want to walk all the way back to you and away from myself. Is this what that "mountain" is all about? Is this the message you are sending me?

> **Dear Child of Mine,**
>
> You can't heal a wound by saying it's not there. You have acknowledged your wound but still need total healing. That's what I am about to do in your life if you permit me. You are ready for the next stop on your pilgrimage. Go to the mountain. Be strong and take heart as you wait for me. *Psalm 27:5, 14*

Chief Sara's Homecoming

The job summons came a week later. So I went to the mountain.

For months I'd cried out in the wee hours of the morning, "Who will take his place?" Forty came to fill that empty space, and what a mixed bag of troubled humanity! Felonies on their way to happen again and again: experimenters with alcohol, glue, drugs; runaways and truants; assaulters with deadly weapons; firesetters; intimidators; suicide risks; uncontrollables—depressed, rejected, abused, abandoned, ego-bankrupted.

Thirty minutes after landing right side up at the foot of Saddle Mountain, I trudged up the trail to meet my first challenge: Eighty-nine pounds of seething anger with no place to go. Alternating between heaving his foot locker and ripping his coat to shreds, Ramon was threatening to run down the mountain "just as soon as dark gets here." Beneath all that motor-mouth overflow, I saw only a scared nine-year-old, hovering between fight and flight. For three solid weeks Ramon hid inside his replaced coat and hood, wearing it everywhere in Indian Summer's heat. Then one glorious morn, and a cool one at that, he shed his coat.

"Chief, how'd you do it?" I gasped to his counselor.

"Oh, I didn't do anything," was the reply. "He just announced he wasn't wearing that hot thing today."

When I first addressed my troops, I captured them with disarming frankness. Mustering my General Patton stance to corral every wandering eyeball, I began:

"Men, you're here because of problems you haven't been able to solve. Furthermore, you think you're the only ones in the world with problems. Well, I've got news for you. Everybody has problems. Just let me tell you some of Chief Sara's problems for the last three and a half years. My mother died unexpectedly of brain cancer. Now I have no parents. My young nephew was killed in a tragic accident. A few months later his dad, my youngest brother, was operated on for a giant malignancy and has now taken the limit of chemotherapy treatments. My dearest friend was hopelessly mangled in an accident shortly after visiting our home and vegetated in a nursing home two years before she died. Then came the final blow, a marriage breakup after nearly twenty-eight years! Try those troubles on for size, fellows. Yes, I wanted to scream and holler, rant and rave, and I did my share of that. You bet I did! Like you, I felt like kicking life in the teeth for handing me such a raw deal. But I had to find a more intelligent way than blowing up and blaming everybody else. That's why I gave up my university teaching and came to

Dear God, I'm Divorced

this mountain. As your educational director, I don't plan to sit around here and dilapidate while listening to my arteries harden. So let's get off our duffs and get our acts together. I don't plan to give you one iota of sympathy—and I want none of yours!"

Pain communicates. Every last boy shook my hand, clumped me on the back, or gave me a quick hug as he filed out the door. "Chief Sara, thanks for telling us. It ain't easy to say those things. We know exactly how you feel," one sniffed.

My prize pupil, also a coat-hugger, arrived three weeks before Thanksgiving. A walking catalogue of all ninety-nine known learning disabilities, this ten-year-old had tried drugs, alcohol, truancy, family intimidation, breaking and entering, and had almost killed his younger sister during a glue-induced hallucination. He had the vocal cords of Michael the Archangel and when his mouth opened, his brain closed down. Just positioning him for a three-minute run put me in competition for the Nobel Peace Prize. Yet, after our candlelit Thanksgiving banquet, he wiped me out by coming up to the Lieutenant Governor of North Carolina and offering his hand for a shake, then turning to me and blurting out, "Chief Sara, you're the most beautiful lady in North Carolina tonight. And shucks, nobody'd even guess you was fifty years old!"

Those boys often brought out my homicidal instincts, but they left me no time for pityitis as I figured out how to outsmart them and make learning a pleasure. One thing was certain: I could have gone anywhere in that woods, day or night, and not have had a hair on my head disturbed. They identified with me.

Taking a week's comp time to teach a gifted course in Florida, I returned to camp exhausted but exhilarated on a

Monday morning. Suddenly a shout that would have disturbed the dead echoed across the mountain. "Welcome home, Chief Sara!" Guitars were readied as my troops sang me a fabulous, original composition of three whole lines. Representatives from all four "tribes" came forth to bow and kiss my hand. No standing ovation here or abroad ever sounded so sweet! When the boys broke into my very favorite, "Amazing Grace," giddy tears of joy coursed down my cheeks. Then came the pronouncement from my prize ten-year-old: "Chief Sara, we ain't gonna let you go off this mountain again. You stayed away too long."

I was home! My tattered humanity had survived as sanity and the rhythms of life returned. Now I could fling away all those tinctured, self-stained emotions as I sank down every night in the corner that housed my bed, experiencing a healthy tiredness born of productivity and usefulness.

Dear God,

When I beheld those ageless mountains and thought of all the storms, howling winds, snow, and floods that had battered them unmercifully, I whispered to myself, "Weary mountains, you are still standing—and by God's grace, so am I."

Thank you, Father, for your amazing grace that filled every crack of my empty heart with a troubled boy. I now resign my charter membership in the Order of Bruised Souls.

Dear Child of Mine,

Did I not tell you that my grace is sufficient for you? Never forget that my strength is made perfect in your weakness. *2 Corinthians 12:9*

And That's What Joy Is!

The night wind howled at our flickering, sputtering lanterns as a lopsided moon lit our path on Saddle Mountain. The chill factor was -35°, and nobody in his right mind should have been out on that frostbitten night, but there we were—scrambling into an unheated, wheezing bus, hoping we wouldn't have to push it down the mountain. While stomping our feet and clapping our hands, we began to warm up our chilled vocal cords. Soon the boys' favorite, "O Freedom, O Freedom" echoed across the frozen heights and wafted skyward.

My eighty-five-year-old landlord, almost totally deaf and trying to outlast his third pacemaker, was first on our Christmas concert route. He thought the angels had descended to his pastures as fifty-two of us trooped up to his front door, greeted him with a few hugs, and sang several hearty selections. When one of the campers presented him with an exquisite "Eye of God," hand-fashioned in red and black yarn, he wept tears of joy.

Next stop was a petite blind lady, followed by five more shut-ins. Chilled to the bone, but hearts skipping with pleasure, we lumbered back up the mountain to a blazing chuck-wagon fire and goodies galore. As was our custom with any field trip, we evaluated this nocturnal happening. First one boy and then another, shyly first, then boldly, verbalized what this event meant to him. Many of them had never been caroling before!

Scottie, who had witnessed his mother choked to death by her lover, stood up a bit timidly, clearing his throat as his Adam's apple seesawed up and down.

"You know," he said, "up until now I thought I knew what joy was. Joy meant someone throwing a big party where we ate everything in sight and got high on whatever was circulating around. Someone else did all the work and footed the bill! Well, tonight, after we sang to that little old blind lady, she insisted on shaking every one of our hands. When I got up next to her, she reminded me so much of my little grandmother that I told myself what she needed was a big bear hug. So I just screwed up my courage and hugged her and she hugged me, and next thing you know we were both doing the jig! And that's what joy is—doing something for someone else to make them happy instead of expecting everybody to hand you out a good time."

There were few dry eyes as wave after wave of applause bounced around the fireside that cold night.

Dear God,

What a special definition of joy from a lad who had known so little of it! Lord Jesus, let my life make a difference with these boys who are so scarred.

My Dear Child,

I cover these boys, who have been judged losers by the world, with my blessings from head to foot! *Proverbs 10:6*

The *Coral Sea*

My eldest departed San Francisco's dawn on that Elmer-glued World War II relic, the *Coral Sea*, carrying seventy-two F-4 fighter jets and an undetermined number of other planes and missiles. Destination: the Indian Ocean and Iranian waters to relieve the *Kitty Hawk*. I know mothers have sent their sons to sea for centuries, but I claimed all 7,600 promises of the Bible for Doug.

When Christmas was celebrated in the Philippines, Doug wrote, "No matter where you are, if you are with a group of Christians you can celebrate Jesus. Some of the boat people came to the air base for the Christmas Eve service and sang 'Amazing Grace,' the only English hymn they knew. It was something to hear! The only refugee who could speak English told how thankful his people were that they had been rescued and could celebrate Christmas in a free country."

Night landings were a hazard on that antiquated tub with limited landing space. My hair stood on end as Doug wrote of one such hairy event when he landed with the equivalent of a quart of gas!

But the tour held many light moments, too. Even the angels must have laughed when Doug broke all jogging records as those mean monkeys chased him in the Philippine Islands. From Thailand he wrote, "We had to watch out for the elephants that were being taken for a walk. It was hard to figure out who was walking whom." Of course, my brave son had to find out what the local economy of each country could offer his stomach after having eaten squid and octopus in Korea.

Occasionally the *Coral Sea* had a few tag skirmishes with the twenty-six sleek Russian warships in the area, any of which was able to blow the *Coral* off the face of the earth. The most difficult period of waiting was three weeks of silence following the aborted rescue attempt of our hostages in Iran. I just gave him to the Lord, as I waited for that letter proclaiming him safe: "Some hours after the rescue attempt, we had an All Alert, Man Your Station command. My F-4 was second off the launching pad. For forty-eight hours our men rotated in escorting the United States ships out of Iranian waters. Never have I been so relieved to land with all our bombs and missiles intact! Mother, I felt your prayer power and the prayers of your friends and your church to such an extent that had my C.O. ordered me to fly to Tehran and back, I would have made it."

Dear God,

There was dancing on the green that great day in June when the *Coral Sea* churned in some two hundred miles from San Diego, and the C.O. allowed his men to fly those birds that last lap home. Thank you for keeping watch over Doug and his comrades. He wrote that those seven months at sea weren't easy and that he "was subjected to temptations" he had never before faced. In the letter I most treasure, he said "I did a good job, thanks to your prayers and the Word of God that I really had a chance to study on this trip. I am coming back to Barbara a much stronger man. Mother, I know everything will work out for our family on God's schedule. We'll just have to hang in there! I love you."

Dear Child of Mine,

Though Douglas rides the morning winds to the farthest oceans, even there my hand will guide him, my strength will support him. *Psalm 139:9*

Dear God, I'm Divorced

Last Day on the Mountain

Too many thoughts were crowding my heart this morning. Chiefest among them was how to tell my forty boys good-bye without breaking down. We had been welded together in a common cause as we arose from our self-pity, despair, subterfuges, and dishonesties. I have long believed that everything that comes into our lives, be it persons or events, must contain something from God to be loved and experienced. And I had loved and experienced these lively troops. Believe me, it had been an *experience*! I'd be wealthy if I had a dime for every time I've uttered, "Why do you think God gave you two ears and only ONE mouth?"

Even after a year, I still marvel at the majesty of dawn on Saddle Mountain. A tumultuous shout of "Good morning, Chief Sara," surged over me as I crept through the gates today. (I was falling apart already and I hadn't even made it out of the car yet!) Reluctantly I had told my troops I was returning to the halls of learning to again train student teachers how to teach kids. "And think how much more I know now after a year with you," I sheepishly explained.

My first gift of the day was a real jewel—one Egg McMuffin and a carton of orange juice. Following it was a warm loaf of banana bread. Next came a beautiful signed pottery gem. At 10 A.M. I was presented with a stained-glass Swedish bluebird of happiness and a huge German chocolate cake. (*Glory be! If this keeps up, they'll roll me off the mountain,* I thought.) On and on it went—small trinkets or scraps of paper with a verse or a sentence for Chief Sara. Just as I'd deceived myself into thinking I was brave enough to make it without bawling, I was summoned to the chuck wagon, where the entire crew was gathered. A spokesman said, "Chief Sara, we don't have the gift of words like you do, so instead of trying to say our appreciation, we're gonna sing it. Is that okay?"

"Yes, as long as you don't sing, 'The Old Gray Mare, She Ain't What She Used to Be!'"

"Why, Chief Sara, how did you guess our first number?"

Oh, those jokesters! The entire group concertized me with "My Eyes Have Seen the Glory," "Go Down, Moses," "O Freedom," "The Five Steps of Camp," "We Shall Overcome," and an all-time original, "Chief Sara, We Love You." They saved my favorite until the last, and "Amazing Grace" really did me in. Wordlessly I hugged every last boy and each staff member as our tears mingled. We'd been certified together in the School of Pain.

My transitional class, feeling so important, carted the last crate of books from my office to the car. Emotionally spent, I had begged to be allowed to go to my car alone. Just as I was trying to decide if the car had room for me, I heard a rustle and a clearing of throats. Out of nowhere came the "tribe" that had most threatened my sanity. Ramon, Andy (formerly the most belligerent boy in camp), and my coat-hugger were clutching a bouquet of wild flowers and thistle. Their message? "We had to say good-bye again. And Chief Sara, don't forget why God gave you two eyes, two ears, and *one* mouth!"

Dear God,

Father, this experience has no price tag. I have been on holy ground. Thank you to eternity for sending me to the mountain!

Dear God, I'm Divorced

My Child,
I have planted these boys on top of this mountain and you have nurtured them in my name. *Ezekiel 17:23.*

Priory Family

Life is full of wonderful surprises!

I completed that 813-mile marathon from Saddle Mountain to St. Petersburg and fell through my foyer, looking like something that rose up from the swamp on a full-moon night. Monday morning I limped into St. Leo at 8 A.M. with seven crates of books. After a week's daily commuting of a hundred miles on the I-75 Grand Prix, I soon wished I were back in the wilderness.

Following the advice of my mentor, I clutched my courage and appeared on the doorstep of the Benedictine Priory, casting myself on the mercy of the Prioress, Sister Jerome Levy. What a combination of wit, intelligence, earthy vitamins, and backbone! I knew right off that no sanctimonious platitudes would ever cross the lips of this veteran teacher. Sister Rosario, who had taken a course from me in one of our Florida Teaching Centers, happened by. "Oh, Sister Jerome, you must get to know Dr. Thrash! This lady knows more about kids and teaching them than anyone." On and on went this unsolicited testimonial—so on September 26 I was adopted by the sisters, becoming their Baptist Benedictine.

I occupied Room 54, the small guest chamber usually assigned to mothers on weekend visits. The spartan single bed, small table, chair, desk, and a tired-looking easy chair suited me perfectly. The bath was an unexpected luxury. Our third floor, a wee United Nations, rippled with bustling activity, especially if the moon was full or exams were pending. Clipped British accents, torrents of Spanish, Southern drawls, and assorted Yankee dialects mingled with blaring stereos and TV commercials.

I put in a twelve-hour day on the campus, except for Wednesdays. Then I joined the sisters at mass, dined with them, and served kitchen duty, where all sorts of jollifications erupted. Wow! Sister Irma was wicked with a wet dish towel, especially when I bent over to stack the plastics! (I told her she must have charmed a million swains during her Texas youth.) Sister Jerome held me captive with tales of her memorable skirmishes in the educational jungle. Sister Rosario always slipped me an extra piece of pie on pecan-pie nights. (Despite my best intentions, it was devoured by midnight.)

The energetic diversity of the sisters was phenomenal. Some were retired and held specific responsibilities in the Priory. The majority of them went out into all walks of life each morning and returned at day's end. Clinics, classrooms, hospitals, libraries, graduate schools, and offices were their workbenches. I shared their visions, victories, setbacks, and needs, and they shared mine.

Dear God,

Thank you, Father, for such a wonderful surprise, bestowed when I needed it the most. What an ecumenical happening for this Baptist Benedictine!

My Child,

The sisters make music for me as they bless so many. In honoring you, they honor me! *Ephesians 5:19–21*

Dear God, I'm Divorced

Experiencing Exeter

God threw out yet another lifeline to me by involving me in Hospital Christian Fellowship, an international, interdenominational organization dedicated to encouraging every Christian caregiver to bring Christian values and principles to patients and fellow health-care workers.

It was a holy day of wonderment there in the Great Hall at Exeter University as I forgot myself and held hands across the world with 1,000 people gathered from 106 nations to proclaim "the King of kings and Lord of lords" at Hospital Christian Fellowship! The awe-inspiring opening ceremony of delegates, in native dress as they placed their flags under the banner of the Great Physician, will be engraved forever on my heart. We were reminded that "the God of the Impossible brought delegates here who, for security's sake, cannot tell you how they came or how they will return." The Polish delegation of six, arriving three days late, received a standing ovation. "Fear Not, I Have Called You by Name," they declared. What more timely theme for me than "Communicating Christ to Broken Lives."

"Bind us together with the cords of love, cords that cannot be broken," reverberated from the eastern-block nations throughout the seven translation booths. Oh, the beautiful raw courage landscaped on the faces of so many from Europe and Africa. Tears streamed down their cheeks as one delegate quietly sang, "He Died for My Tears." The simplicity of their prayers, testifying to their absolute dependence on the Lord, sank deeply into my heart. "Boldly claim a promise of God and refuse to let go of that promise until it is fulfilled in your life!" they were affirming.

A light touch was provided by a visit from the Children's Choir of Taiwan, who were on European concert tour. They stole our hearts with Handel's "Largo" and the theme song from "Love Story," then proceeded to bring the house down with "Oh, Susanna." (Days later Americans were still chuckling over their enunciation of "Alabama" and "banjo.")

A little Jesuit priest from Yugoslavia reminded those of us from the U.S. of our mixed-up priorities: "You have too many things, too much disposable junk passing through your lives. We have been bombed out so many times, leaving our cities with what we possessed on our backs, that we have no more sense than to trust God to care for us. But you Americans trust in things."

I believe God brought me to Exeter to hear Dr. Bruce Thompson's messages on forgiveness:

"God can reach back into the storehouse of your life and heal your wounds. With his scalpel, God opens up a deep hurt in your spirit and it bleeds. All the while, he's pouring his love on that wound. When you bring that wound to the surface and surrender it to him to heal, Jesus will lift it out, bear it, and release it, bringing a new dimension to your life. In bearing that wound away, he sends his healing process. As Isaiah 53 so beautifully puts it, He is the specialist in wounded spirits. When Jesus bears that wound, he gives us insights into the person who has wounded us, allowing us to see that one's heart. Often that person is Jesus' lost lamb, too, with a trampled spirit. We enter the door of God's kingdom through forgiveness. Our bodies are delicately, intricately designed, and we cannot be whole until we have for-

Dear God, I'm Divorced

given. Forgiveness is the greatest therapy we can offer anyone. 'Forgive as ye have been forgiven.'"

The second Sunday's service, "Communicating the Christ Life," was followed by Holy Communion, a dress rehearsal for heaven. Forty doctors from many nations passed the loaves of bread and the goblets of wine. Our founder, Frances Grimm, reminded us, "There are four chairs on the platform, but only three are occupied. This is not by accident. Jesus is here today in our midst—loving, touching, healing."

"What a Friend We Have in Jesus," "Amazing Grace," and "Because He Lives" shook the rafters of the Great Hall. While passing the goblets, the doctors broke out spontaneously in "O Come Let Us Adore Him." I thought I'd died and gone to heaven!

Dear God,

Before returning to England, I once again experienced such deep, searing sorrow and brokenness that I was almost destroyed. Yet now, as I sit in your presence, I find only my "shallowness" has been destroyed. Sara Arline Cate Thrash is still crying out, "Lord, I believe; help thou my unbelief!" But you always come to me, walking on the water. Beloved Father, like Mary I cry out, "My soul doth magnify the Lord, and my spirit rejoices in God my Savior!

Dear Child of Mine,

My only Son prayed, "Father forgive them. . . . Into your hands I commit my spirit." You are learning. *Luke 23:34, 46*

Haunting Eyes

Scurrying across England to catch the night ship to Holland for some R and R, I was haunted by the tired eyes of one woman on the train who told us her husband was dying of leukemia, his suffering compounded by crippling arthritis. As she quietly spoke of her isolation, her desolation, my heart heard more than she was verbalizing. She was so people-hungry, so touch-starved. Taking another cigarette from a crumpled pack, she spoke as if to herself: "Oh, I know I smoke far too much, although I never smoke in the same room with my husband. But what's left in life for me but a few smokes?"

When my transfer city was announced, that dear lady jumped up and helped me off the train, even unscrewing my sagging luggage cart and rebalancing my two protesting bags. I took her hand and squeezed it gently as I whispered, "Thank you. Thank you so much! You beautiful English people are so helpful to confused Americans like me."

But what I really wanted to do was wrap my arms around her and lay my cheek against hers. It would have been presumptuous to tell her that there was more to her life than a few smokes. However, I *could* have said, "Dear friend, I care about you. Would you give me your address? I want to write you when I get back home."

Dear God,
Why didn't I say that?

My Child,
 Inasmuch as you have encouraged the least of my children, you have encouraged me. Arline, what have you learned from this experience? *Matthew 25:35–40*

Hello, Holland!

There she was—Holland on a full-mooned night! I could hardly contain myself. Where were the windmills, tulips, and wooden shoes? Bear hugs all around at Hoek van Holland, as H.C.F. delegate Phyllis tells her Brian, "Honey man, look who's coming to dinner—and breakfast and lunch—for a few days!" We part company with other delegates and two hours later devour breakfast under the watchful eyes of a green parrot, who flies about in the quaint little restaurant. It is there I nod to my first windmill.

What a charming, old-world cottage and garden is Phyllis and Brian's snug habitat on the Netherlands-German border. Phyllis coos to all the plants inside and out as Brian, with a proper touch of modesty, shows her all the impossibilities he has wrought about the house in her two-week absence. She throws her arms about him and swoons appreciatively as I suggest that maybe I'd best become the cook.

Today has been an unforgettable experience. We traveled thirty-five miles to an English-speaking church, Shalom House, which meets in a three-storied mansion in the woods. Before we began the trip, Brian, this top-notch engineer, who'd been a Christian only two years, bowed his head in that little Volks and quietly prayed, "You know there will be so many people on the road today, Lord. Be my eyes, be my ears, be my brain, my reflexes." What beautiful lessons in faith's simplicity from this special couple!

The young man directing the music at Shalom House had been stationed at MacDill Airforce Base in Tampa, seventeen miles from my home. I marvel at our small world—New Zealand, Maine, and Chicago were also represented. The pastor's young son accompanied the pianist on the violin, after which the entire congregation gave a "big clap" to God for what he has done in our lives. Several men and women spoke quietly of the Almighty's blessings and direction, even in the face of many reversals, adversity, and illnesses.

The pastor then spoke the Word, and it brought the Lord's blazing light into our midst. After Bible study, led by the pastor's wife in an upper bedroom, a picnic awaited us, and children spilled out boisterously from everywhere after two hours' captivity. I had spoken briefly during the Bible-study hour, and the visitor from Maine touched my arm. "Sara, you have the priceless gift of laughter, with which you made two excellent points. I'm going to use your examples on my Anglican congregation when I return home. Don't ever lose that gift in your teaching." How grateful I was for that unexpected affirmation!

Dear God,

Our return trip was bittersweet, Father. First we stood in silent tribute by row after row of crosses in Arnhem, where thirty thousand Canadians in one week were lost at the hands of the Germans in World War II. But next came the merry sight of a bride and groom racing from a church to celebrate life. My heart bursts in gratitude for this rarefied Sunday!

Dear God, I'm Divorced

The End-of-the-Day Vase

Glory be! I spied it in the window of a German
antique shop—an end-of-the-day vase perched on a bale
of hay. If only best friend Sara, who had introduced me
to such a treasure, were here to see this one! Very
patiently she had explained the concept to her unenlight-
ened companion, "Arline, at the end of each day the potter
flings all the leftover dyes into one container, stirs and
swirls them about with abandon, and uses that extraor-
dinary combination of pigment to tint or stain a vase.
Thus its name, end of the day, denotes the vase as cre-
ated with leftovers, the remnants of a day's labor.
Sometimes it is a calamity of uninviting colors, but more
often it is a blend of exquisite shadings and commands a
respectable price."

This particular tiny gem commanded only thirty-five dollars, but the more I studied it, the more beauty I beheld.

Dear God,
How often our lives are governed and colored as end-of-the-
day vases. Unforeseen detours tinge our horizons. Depending
on how we use them, those experiences have the capacity to
become either catastrophic calamities or subtle blends of unexpected beauty. You, the master potter, can take any cir-

cumstance and shape it into an exquisite vessel if we give you permission to do so.

My Child,
Behold, I make all things new and wonderful.
Revelation 21:5

"Forgive and Remember..."

Here I sit on the gate to a silently beautiful family burial plot, hoping the German owner doesn't come out and shoot me for trespassing. I first spied the old chapel with its stately steeple on a jogging trek. Upon closer examination, I discovered that the ancient house of worship was attached to the family dwelling, which resembles a country hotel.

Now meditating in this oasis, I am reminded of the words of that Italian friar, Savonarola, who was tortured for his unswerving faith and reforming zeal, eventually perishing at the stake. "Do not forgive and forget; forgive and remember" he said. The only true forgiveness is to remember and *still* forgive:

"If you remember and at the same time forgive, really forgive, you'll succeed in accomplishing an emotional overcoming, a spiritual discipline. If you forgive and forget in the usual sense, you're just driving what you remember into the subconscious; it stops there and festers. But to look, even regularly, upon what you remember, and know you have forgiven, is achievement. First you don't forgive at all, then you make a sacrificial gesture of trying to forgive. You tell yourself to forget. Finally you forgive and remember what you've forgotten—and nevertheless forgive!"

How I wish I'd stumbled upon those words years ago or heard them from some pulpit! For Savonarola pinpoints the very stages I've agonized through—the nonforgiving stage; the pious, sacrificial gesturing stage; and finally the forgiving-and-remembering stage. When Jesus answered Peter's question about how many times he must forgive, he must have had me in mind. "Seventy times seven." That's how many times Satan dredges up the past and throws it in my face, and how many times I must again hand that hurt over to my Lord.

"Forgiveness is the scent of the violet on the heel that crushed it" (Mark Twain). I doubt that Saul of Tarsus ever forgot that look on Stephen's face as he was murdered. Long before Saul was clobbered by that divine two-by-four on the Damascus Turnpike, he had to grapple with the memory of Stephen's face, shining with glory, and his quiet prayer, "Father, do not hold this sin against them." I believe Saul's undoing began the very moment of Stephen's outpouring of forgiveness upon his enemies.

Dear God,

This glorious day I allow you to lift my wound and bear it away, thereby releasing me from its pain and healing me, even though some scarring remains. Remember when I was barely three and I stood too close to our fireplace and was burned? To this day I bear the scars of third-degree burns on my back and right arm. That pain happened. It was real, as is the memory that was etched in my young mind. Likewise there remains scar tissue long after our emotional wounds have been cleansed and healed.

Lord Jesus, I fling the last vestige of unforgiveness across this gate and into this burial plot. And when Satan tries to dredge it up, I'll remind him I have given it a decent burial in a far-off country. Now I'll skedaddle off this gate before I end up in the family burial plot, too.

Dear Child,

Forgiveness is not optional for those who call me Father. Your own soul is nourished when you cast the bread of forgiveness among those who have wronged you. Be kind and compassionate to others, even as my beloved Son forgave you. *Ephesians 4:31–32*

In a Dutch Garden

I awakened today to the second most beautiful sound on earth—the laughter of children. On this glorious morn it was Dutch children clomping right under my window en route to their first day of school. So they *do* wear wooden shoes! In the afternoon I loped three miles across the German border to attend a small fair where screaming *kinder* careened on a music-filled carousel and fat ducks wandered about for a handout. Later, dusk caught me on a ten-speed, silhouetted against the Rhine. Now the haunting afterglow is hoarded in my host's garden, where the evening star appears as big as my fist. So many significant events have taken place in gardens. The human race began in a beautiful garden. Resurrection's glory burst forth in one, too.

Exactly two years ago I bowed my head outside a judge's chamber and wept as if the tears would never stop. There was no beauty then, no reasoning out the situation, no prayers left in me. But shining crowns are cast in red-hot crucibles. And I realize now that God never left the crucible of my life unattended. He was there, observing the refiner's fire the whole time, deeply touched by my infirmity. That kind of love does not preclude pain, but it walks right beside us in our agony.

The Scots have a quaint saying when they happen upon an accident: "Sir, you and the road have parted!" All of us have parted from the road many times. We have wandered far from the Creator's plan. At one time or another in our lives, we seek the nobility we have lost. Then we must go back to where that loss occurred, where we fell down. Like David of old, we must repent, confess our failure, ask forgiveness, and get up again.

Dear God,

Thank you, Father, for lifting me from failure and carrying me back to your fold. In this quiet garden your presence surrounds me with peace. I take my hostess's hand and brush my lips across the slash marks on her wrists—scars inflicted over a decade ago when a husband deserted his wife and young daughter. "Dear friend, God has healed your wounds, too."

We who have suffered deeply are welded together in a bond of understanding incomprehensible to those who have never known such pain.

My Child,

I will never abandon you or leave you as an orphan in the storm. Always, in every circumstance, I will come to you. *John 14:18*

It's Hard to
Kill Us Cates Off!

I last saw my younger brother, James Douglass, in his driveway on an August Sunday. He had survived the removal of a massive malignancy months before and battled his way back to work inch-by-inch through a maze of chemotherapy sessions. Giving me a hearty farewell salute late that August day, he drawled, "Sis, I'm gonna make it. It's hard to kill us Cates off!"

James fought as valiantly as Mama when that dreaded cancer invaded his bloodstream. A year later he was still working, even though sight in one eye was affected and he could barely endure a shortened workday. He and Lila had a last vacation touring Florida. Despite inheriting an overabundance of Daddy's absentminded chromosomes, James remembered Lila's Christmas request and presented it to her on their final Christmas, spent in Mississippi with Lila's family.

In our last telephone conversation, James kept repeating, "I'm gonna lick this, Sis." He began a long letter, which was never completed, to Douglas, with whom there was an inseparable bond from my son's early years. Actually, I never knew whom to scold the most when they threw firecrackers under cows one Fourth of July!

As the cancer moved upward to his neck and ears, James went again to Fort Sanders for his final stay. When a young teenager with leukemia came to share the semi-private room, James told him immediately, "I've got cancer, but I'm doing everything the doctor told me to do and I can't afford to get worried and upset. I need my rest, so I

Dear God, I'm Divorced

plan to sleep tonight and I hope you can, too." My brother was a testimony in tenacity and courage to Lila, his children, the medical staff, and the many friends who came to cheer him but went away being cheered themselves.

During Lila's final visit, James somewhat abruptly called to her, "Lila, come sit on my bed a minute." Gently he took her hand, smiled at her, and lifted her hand to pat his right cheek in the exact manner Mama had farewelled him. This was his good-bye to Lila, and it said everything he had left unspoken before.

Dear God,
Father, I think of James each time I read the Indian version of the Twenty-third Psalm. "He enters all the rooms of my heart. He puts his hand on my head and all my tiredness is gone." Were I allowed a peek at the Big House, I daresay I would see Uncle Jim surrounded by a circle of children, telling them of his and Doug's antics on the Fourth of July.

> **Dear Child of Mine,**
> James is right here with me in the place I prepared for him. *John 14:2–3*

Kitchen Benediction

The greatest gift a single parent can give his or her child is permission to love the absentee parent unconditionally. If this is denied, the child will find a way to love and defend the absentee anyway. You can remove a parent from the home, but you can't take a parent from a child's heart. On the other hand, giving your child permission to love that parent is an act of casting your bread upon the waters and having it return to you toasted, buttered, and jellied.

What a return on my investment I had this past Mother's Day! Mark slipped into the kitchen on Saturday a bit sheepishly and heaved a huge pink hydrangea plant onto the counter. Before I could exclaim, "Why, Son, that's beautiful, and a whole day early, too," God stilled my overactive tongue as oft he does.

"How do you like it, Mom? I bought it at Albertson's for Diane (his stepmom). Figured she'd never had a Mother's Day gift before. Even got a card to go with it." Whipping out a card from behind his back, he handed it to me. The card pictured a grubby little boy on the front. Inside it read, "What's a Mom like you doing with a Kid like me?" With a bit of hesitation Mark said, "Thought I'd give it to Dad tonight and ask him to present it to Diane tomorrow."

Tears dotted my eyes as I realized the risk Mark had taken in showing his present to me and the silent compliment he had paid me in daring to believe I would accept both him and his gift to his stepmom. We looked at each other, then wordlessly threw our arms about each other. Finally Mark said, "Hey Mom! We've both come a long way, haven't we?"

Dear God,

My heart sang of this kitchen benediction! My son had put a halo on our day as he reminded me of the preciousness of life and forgiveness.

Dear Child of Mine,

You have learned an invaluable lesson. Whatever you bind on earth shall be bound in heaven. Whatever you free on earth will be freed in heaven. *Matthew 18:18*

Dear God, I'm Divorced

What Did I Learn?

After our offspring had weathered a setback or disaster, whether it was of their own making or another's, we elders would ask them, "What did you learn from this experience?" Oft-times at one of the way stations or rest stops on my pilgrimage, I have heard God's voice in quietness ask me, "Arline, what did you learn from this experience?" Now I can answer:

1. *Taking God's love for granted is self-defeating.* I've suffered from spiritual amnesia when it came to his sense of justice. I cannot be permitted to get away with disobedience and rebellion anymore than I could allow my children to do so. He asked me time and time again, "Why call ye me Lord and do not the things I say?" God always deals with me constructively, productively, and redemptively, even though I shrink from the experience. Yet the very thing I run from in terror or rebellion is the thing that will make me grow. Like Job, I've often allowed my suffering to embitter me toward the only One who could deliver me.
2. *Grief is work, but it must be done.* The more preoccupied I am with only my misery, the more attention I give it, the less likely I will heal. In time every wound will heal if I let God help. My attitude is the key: "Do I want to be healed?"
3. *When I demand explanations or answers to*

my questions, God is silent in his love. Moses reminds us, "The secret things belong to the LORD our God; but the things revealed belong to us . . ." (Deut. 29:29). God tells me as much as he wants me to know. I've found out the hard way I can live without understanding everything, but I can't live without the Lord's presence. I choose the latter.

4. *Forgiveness is not optional.* If I do not forgive, by God's very nature he cannot offer to me what I am unwilling to offer to another. When Job forgave his friends and prayed for them, the Lord restored Job. Forgiveness is a self-cleaning oven that must be used daily.

5. *No love is ever wasted.* Willard, father of our children, is now my brother in Christ. For him and Diane, his wife, I wish all good things.

6. *In my pilgrimage I must make many in-flight corrections.* When I get off target, it is the Spirit who convicts me, not some Bible-waving saint! I shall forever refrain from that fruitless exercise. When I pass through deep waters and great trouble, God will be with me. When I plunge through rivers of difficulty, I will not drown! When I enter the fire of oppression, I will not be burned up; the flames will not consume me. For God—my Lord, my Savior, the Holy One—is with me. I will not be afraid (Isa. 43:2–3, 5).

Dear God,

Father, I'm one satisfied customer! Thank you for forgiving pasts and specializing in futures!

Dear God, I'm Divorced

Dear Child of Mine,
I shall lead you home with great care. You will walk beside the quiet stream and not stumble. For I am your Father. *Jeremiah 31:9*

Afterglow

The pain of any loss lessens and at times disappears entirely. Yet it resurfaces briefly at unexpected moments as vividly as ever. This is not to say that my grief process was unsuccessful. Rather, it says that joy and sorrow often cohabit. I will never fully recover from my loss until I cross over to the Big House. There are some things our fix-it society simply can't repair. The pain, however, is now a gentle, kind pinch, never quite allowing me to forget the fragility of my humanity, the vulnerability of my heart. To make peace with pain is not to deny or erase what once was. Each time I look at the tall frame of the son who most resembles his father, I am reminded briefly of what once was. But it is a joyous, peaceful remembering, though tinged with a trace of sadness. I am more gentle and patient with myself than I once was. Losses interrupt our plans; they change us and alter forever the course of our lives.

The father of my children came one Saturday morning to tell me he would remarry the following month. No one except God was there as I slipped back into darkness. But grief scholar Lindemann reminds us that it is up to us "to find a way to replace that which at first seems irreplaceable."

Suffering has the possibility of teaching, tempering, and gentling as no other experience can. When we give God permission to walk by our side through this suffering, pain can be transformed into a source of new life, new direction. From the abyss, Nietzsche proclaimed, "That which does not kill you strengthens you."

How vividly I remember the night of Mark's ordination to the ministry. Divinity waged a fierce war with my dusty humanity and won a week before, when I graciously invited Willard and Diane to join other family members and out-of-town guests in a celebratory dinner after the service. They graciously accepted. Near midnight, after all the guests had departed, my dearest friend and co-hostess threw her arms about me and we had a good weep. "Oh, Arline, I could never have asked my former husband and his wife to share such an event with me. How could you, how could you?"

How could I not?

Dear God,

During the last five years, you and I have walked together in sixteen nations and crossed and recrossed the United States. Everywhere broken and hurting people have asked the same question: "Will it ever stop hurting?" To all of them I owe an honest answer, albeit I can only speak through the lens of my own experience. Father, this is what I've said. Am I on target?

My Dear Child,

You have been abandoned, forsaken, tossed with the tempest, grieved in spirit like a wife of one's youth who is rejected, cast off. But fear not! Do not live in shame. I, your Creator, will be your husband.

Extend your boundaries, hold back nothing. I will rebuild you on foundations of sapphires with stones of turquoise and walls of precious jewels. *Isaiah 54:1–8, 11–12*

Epilogue

Dear Mom,

Just a line to say thanks.

You have done so much for me, for all of us.

You are the inspiration that keeps me going.

You have been through so much, and yet your smile always shines through.

All my friends say you are the greatest lady they know, and even though I just seem to take you for granted, I feel the same way they do.

So this is just a letter saying THANKS. I love you.

Your greatest admirer, your son,
David

"By his stripes we are healed."
By our wounds others are healed.